GOVERNMENT INTERVENTION AND INDUSTRIAL POLICY

STUDIES IN THE BRITISH ECONOMY

General Editor: Derek Lee

Government Intervention and Industrial Policy

SECOND EDITION

by
Allen Skuse,
Head of Economics,
Haberdashers' Aske's (Hatcham) Boys' School

HEINEMANN EDUCATIONAL BOOKS
LONDON

Heinemann Educational Books Ltd
22 Bedford Square, London WC1B 3HH

LONDON EDINBURGH MELBOURNE AUCKLAND
HONG KONG SINGAPORE KUALA LUMPUR
NEW DELHI IBADAN NAIROBI JOHANNESBURG
EXETER (NH) KINGSTON PORT OF SPAIN

ISBN 0 435 84556 X

© Allen Skuse 1970, 1972

First published 1970
Second edition 1972
Reprinted 1976, 1978, 1980

To Christine

Printed in Great Britain by
Richard Clay (The Chaucer Press) Ltd,
Bungay, Suffolk

PREFACE

Most economics textbooks attempt to cover the subject within a single volume and in consequence some topics are treated briefly: often these same topics are those whose subject matter changes most rapidly. At present, in order to keep up to date in the field of economics recourse must be made to a vast field of diffused literature including bank reviews, government publications, newspapers and various journals. With these problems in mind this series was conceived. The series consists of specialized books on those topics which are subject to frequent change or where the sources of information are too scattered to be readily available to the average student. It is intended that each book will be revised at frequent intervals in order to take account of new developments.

In such a series, where each book deals with a particular aspect of the economy, there is the inevitable problem that associated topics will be mentioned but not fully explained. It is useful, therefore, if the reader has an idea of what he can expect to find covered explicitly, and it is for this reason that the following outline of the contents of this book is given.

A history of government intervention in general is given, and this includes coverage of the pre-nineteenth-century development towards *laissez-faire*, the doctrine of State non-interference. Too often treatments of the Government's economic role begin with the middle of the nineteenth century, with the implication that intervention is a twentieth-century innovation, which is of course untrue. The general nature of the history up to the 1914–18 War provides the background, not only for this book, concerned as it is with industrial policy, but for other books in the series where other aspects of government policy are examined. For the rest of the book the approach is restricted to the Government's policy as it affects industry. In dealing with government economic responsibility since the last war, emphasis is given to the direct controls of the immediate post-war period, the reaction against these in the early nineteen fifties, the planning controversy and the new machinery of management developed throughout the nineteen sixties, and finally the present Government's policy of less central direction and control. Although monetary and

PREFACE

fiscal measures are described, since they are important instruments
of government control affecting the economic climate in which
industry exists, their theoretical background is left to a further book
to be produced in this series.

I thank John Wiles for preparing the index, and my wife not only
for reading the final draft of the book and making many useful
suggestions but also for her patience.

Allen Skuse

NOTE ON SECOND EDITION (1972)

Apart from minor revisions throughout, this edition includes an
amended Chapter 8, Planning for Growth, covering the period
1962–70, and a completely new ninth chapter, Towards a New Style
of Government, covering the first two years of the Conservative
Government which came to power in 1970.

CONTENTS

1.
HISTORY OF GOVERNMENT
INTERVENTION BEFORE 1870

Foreign trade regulations

By the middle of the eighteenth century the State had established a complex web of *ad hoc* trade regulations based on the various, and sometimes overlapping, policies designed to strengthen the power of the nation and those who ruled it. The resulting regulations fell into four main categories.

Revenue raising

Norman Kings had inherited rights to levy tolls on trade and this process of revenue collection continued as successive monarchs struggled to gather funds in order to wage their wars and maintain their courts and administration. The passing of power from Crown to Parliament made little difference to the need for revenue, and many of the taxes on trade were retained.

Protection of domestic manufacturers

As early as 1463 an Act of Parliament reflected the feeling that English workers' livelihoods could be jeopardized by the import of foreign manufactures, and much of the legislation considered below was introduced partially in an attempt to provide a 'resolute and brutal protection of native industries and native agriculture'.[1]

Political measures to strengthen England and weaken her rivals

The Navigation Acts of 1651 and 1660 gave English ships a monopoly of imperial trade in an attempt to reduce the commercial power of the Dutch. The harm done to the Dutch as a result is in fact doubtful, since it is most likely that English ships would have been mainly responsible for such trade in any case. An example of the effective use of nationalist policy concerns Ireland. The first Restoration Subsidy Act of 1660 introduced taxation on Irish woollens and other

---

[1] Sir John Clapham, *A Concise Economic History of Britain*.

manufactures and there followed a series of measures in the next twenty years which ended Ireland's exports of butter, cattle and meat. In 1670 it was decided that 'enumerated' goods (see below) should not be landed in Ireland. In 1699 the export of Irish manufactures of wool to foreign countries and the colonies was forbidden; they could only come to England where there was no fear of competition from this cheaper cloth in the domestic market.

Mercantilism
The generally held belief that increased national wealth resulted from the enterprise of her merchants as they brought vast quantities of gold into the country meant that the State's function in the sixteenth and seventeenth centuries was felt to be the protection and encouragement of such enterprise. The doctrine of mercantilism, as it was known, was thus responsible for much commercial legislation.

The Staple Act of 1663 required all European goods destined for the colonies to pass through England, which also became the compulsory distribution centre for various 'enumerated' goods such as sugar, tobacco, cotton and ginger, produced on the plantations. The Crown had previously raised much of its money from the taxing of staple exports, but it was now agreed that these should be free of tax as should imports of raw materials, and further that the import of all manufactured goods should be discouraged. In 1691 export duties on such things as pork, beef and butter were removed and 1699 saw the end of duties on, for example, all manufactures of wool, meat, and bread. From 1709 coal could be exported duty free provided it was carried in British ships. The removal of export duties was virtually completed by Walpole in 1721. Britain's trade balance was very much in surplus at the beginning of the eighteenth century, although the degree to which trade regulation was responsible for this is questionable. What cannot be denied, however, is that the trading pattern was distorted by the various measures imposed, whatever the motive for their imposition.

Internal policy
The State did not restrict its interference to foreign trading. Measures which sought to increase the internal mobility of the country's resources and encourage their combination were introduced to increase the national wealth, and, implicitly, to provide increased revenue. The Statute of Artificers of 1563 governing conditions of employment, and the Statute of 1601 re-enacting the Poor Law code

drawn up three years earlier, are perhaps the most famous examples of the legislation which stretched from earliest Elizabethan times to the outbreak of the Civil War, and which formed a comprehensive, if confused, system of industrial and social law. Thus up to the end of the eighteenth century the State felt it to be its duty to encourage, coerce and control various sectors of the economy as it followed policies felt to be in the national interest at any particular point in time.

Changing circumstances, changing views

But circumstances were changing. By the end of the century Britain's technological advances had already put her ahead of her continental rivals, and world trade had expanded. Trading policies, based on the needs of domestic industry protection, political supremacy and the desire to accumulate treasure, were thus beginning to seem out of date, if not impracticable, especially in the eyes of the new capitalist entrepreneurs responsible for the country's development as an industrial as well as a commercial State. This view gained respectability with the appearance of a new 'literature of economics', the content of which showed a marked contrast from traditional thinking. The most important of these works was written by Adam Smith and first published in 1776.[1]

Smith was originally a philosopher who belonged to the naturalist school. In simple terms he believed human conduct to be the result of such compensatory motives as self-love and sympathy. Each individual should thus be free to pursue his own interest, which would at the same time give rise to the furtherance of the common good, because the natural order, promoted by such well-balanced inclinations, is superior to any order artificially created by man. The application of these ideas to economics is obvious. The Government has an essentially passive role, as the common good, in this case increased national wealth, is maximized if each individual is free to follow his own interest, although Smith did in fact concede that it was the duty of the Government to provide for defence, the administration of justice and such institutions as would not exist for lack of adequate profit (he cited education, and the construction of roads, bridges, canals and harbours). Specialization, which greatly increases output, and its necessary complement, exchange, clearly illustrate self-interest and dependence automatically working for the

---

[1] *An Inquiry into the Nature and Causes of the Wealth of Nations.*

common good. Just as there should be no impediment to free exchange between individuals, neither should there be interference by government in free exchange between nations. Just as regulations concerning wages, apprenticeships and other aspects of production involving government support for monopolistic practice interfered with the accumulation of domestic wealth resulting from free competition, so, Smith argued, did regulation of foreign trade act as such a limit internationally. Although such *laissez-faire*[1] arguments attacking mercantilism had in fact often been anticipated, they gained a new force from their context.

Free competition implies, of course, that no one section of the economy should be given protection by the State. Smith therefore argued against the privileged position of agriculture, the result of a Parliament disproportionately endowed with the landed aristocracy. But if he seemed to champion the industrial class against the land-owner it was only that he saw the privileged position of the latter as an obstacle to the growth of industrial capitalism, which both by definition and in practice meant a slower rate of growth of *national* wealth.

Changing policies

The first statesman to accept the need for liberalization of economic policy was William Pitt, who in the ten years before the outbreak of war with France in 1793 had introduced various measures to reduce tariffs. The war, however, reinforced the old arguments for the manipulation of trade as a means to international supremacy, and Britain's trading policies remained virtually intact well into the nineteenth century. During this time, however, mainly by their policy of ploughing back profits, the manufacturers had established Britain as an industrial nation. The competitive advantage over foreign rivals who were not yet industrialized, the repeated failure in trade in the post-war years, the rising productivity of British labour, all these combined to reinforce in their minds the need for new commercial policies which would open up markets. In particular, the industrialists argued against the landowners, since agricultural protection, which kept out primary produce from Europe, reduced the possibility of exporting manufactured goods to that area.

In turn their arguments were supported by the knowledge that the

---

[1] A phrase associated with the Physiocrats, a group of French philosophers who also advocated non-intervention by the State.

population was increasing, as had been predicted by Malthus at the turn of the century. Industrial growth was necessary therefore to provide the increased employment opportunities demanded by an expanding labour force. Although this was a long-run argument (there was much short-run unemployment as the economy adjusted to industrialization) it was none the less a valid one.

Thus the pressure created by the manufacturing classes, and the need to provide employment combined with the now accepted philosophy of economic liberalism to sweep away regulation and restriction, protection and privilege, and provide the economic climate of *laissez-faire* in which Britain expanded to dominate the world by her industry in the second half of the nineteenth century. The task was made easier by the obsolescence of much of the machinery of central and local government and the attitude of the ruling aristocrats who were more concerned with their private estates, local magistracies, party politics, war and foreign policy than with their changing responsibilities as Britain evolved into an industrial State.

Towards free trade

The work begun by Pitt before the Napoleonic Wars was continued by William Huskisson, President of the Board of Trade from 1823–8. Gradually tariffs were reduced by the Whig Chancellors of the 1830s and by Sir Robert Peel in the early 1840s. In 1842 Sir Robert Peel reintroduced Income Tax as a means of compensating for the resulting loss of revenue. But the biggest single obstacle to free trade, the protection of agriculture, still remained. Under the old system agricultural protection had been vital; a self-sufficient nation had less need to import, less to fear in time of war. Protection was now, however, a constraint on the growth of industrial exports. Agriculture was protected by the Corn Laws which limited foreign competition by the imposition of a heavy import duty whenever the domestic price of corn fell below a certain level. The Act of 1815 had been passed in an endeavour to keep the price of corn at its wartime level. Adjustments were made in the 1820s and finally by Peel in 1842 as wheat prices continued to fluctuate, but protection was the motive throughout.

The feelings against agricultural protection were intensified by trade depression in Lancashire in 1839 which led to the formation of the Anti-Corn Law League. Leading the movement were Richard Cobden and John Bright, members representing the urban middle-classes in a Parliament extended in representation by the 1832 Reform

Act. It was pressure of circumstances that forced Peel, against the interests of his own party, to repeal the Corn Laws in 1846. In the autumn of 1845 the potato harvest failed in Ireland, and in the next year British ports were freely opened to the import of foreign wheat as a means of alleviating the effects of the consequent famine. The pressure of public opinion led by the Anti-Corn Law League was enough to ensure that agricultural protection was not reintroduced.

The movement to free trade continued rapidly after this. In 1849, with the repeal of the Navigation Acts, the British shipowner was no longer protected against foreign shipping either in home waters or in trade with the colonies. The colonial pattern was further broken in 1853 with the removal by Gladstone of much of the tariff preferences for colonial products. A bilateral treaty signed with France in 1860, together with the Budget of that and the succeeding year, left Britain free from almost all protection. The spread across Europe of reductions in tariffs, admittedly in the main by reciprocal arrangement, together with the growth of national wealth in Britain in the 1860s, seemed conclusively to prove the effectiveness of free trade. Certainly it was now the accepted policy of both political parties. When the American prairies began to provide enough cheap wheat to cause depression in agriculture at home in the 1870s, Disraeli refused to reintroduce agricultural protection, although he had been its defender some thirty years before.

Internal developments
The policy of State non-intervention was not applied so vigorously domestically, for while old laws were repealed if they were thought to be inconsistent with free contract between individuals, new legislation was enacted protecting the individual against what Smith had called 'untutored self-interest'. In any case individual freedom did not mean that society became atomistic. For various reasons there was a considerable degree of collectivism in the institutions which developed through the middle years of the nineteenth century, some of it encouraged by the State. Neither did the State restrict itself to protective legislation for the 1860s saw the beginnings of the ultimate in State intervention; State enterprise.

Towards freedom of contract
Examples of legislation which set out to free the labour market are;
(i) the Act of 1813 which repealed statutes giving local magistrates

the power to enforce minimum wages, a power they had had since Elizabethan times, and (ii) the most famous, the repeal of the Combination Acts in 1824. There had been laws against collective action since medieval times, but the particular legislation affected had been introduced in 1799 and 1801. Under these Acts combination by either employers or workers was made illegal, although the Acts were only used against the workers, as might be expected from the fact that they were prompted partly by fear of revolution on the French pattern. The aim of the 1824 Repeal Act was to make unions unnecessary by providing a free market in labour. However, as a reaction to the militancy and collective action of workers, an amending Act was introduced in 1825 making trade combination a criminal conspiracy under common law. In practice collective action by both sides of industry continued to grow, albeit outside the law.

The Poor Law Amendment Act of 1834 can also be considered in this context. With limited funds and administrative ability the parishes had been increasingly unable to fulfil a responsibility, originally given them in Tudor times, of caring for those, including the aged, the sick and the insane, who were unable to work, while providing work for the able-bodied unemployed and apprenticeships for the orphans of the parish. Relief had been given both within the recipients' own homes and also in the parish workhouse. In practice the workhouse became a poorhouse where all categories of pauper might find themselves. An Act of 1782 had given parishes the power to combine into unions in order to pool resources. It was also hoped that the workhouses would, as had been the original intention, become places for those who could not work, while the able-bodied poor could be given employment outside the workhouse, with wages being supplemented from local rates. In fact little was done, the war with France both distracting attention and providing employment for the next thirty years.

The 1834 Act proposed the end of outdoor relief for the able-bodied, for it was felt that such provision interfered with the labour market, enabling employers to pay low wages knowing that these would be supplemented from the rates, and encouraging the labourer to be content with casual rather than permanent employment. To 'encourage' the worker to find work outside the workhouse, the conditions inside were made as grim as possible. Underlying this policy, of course, was the faith in the ability of industrial capitalism to provide the necessary employment. And in the long run, with the building of the railways as the major immediate contributor, it can be argued that it did.[1]

Protective legislation

Inherent in the growth of industry, however, was the development of the large-scale industrial community, and this gave rise to a concentration of bad conditions for which there had been no precedent. The severity of these conditions was enough to persuade even the most ardent individualist that the State had a role to play here. It took time, however, for what has been called the 'new paternalism' to develop. For it had to fight the vested interest of the vast majority of manufacturers[2] whose position coincided so well with the philosophy of individual freedom and State non-intervention.

The first laws dealing with conditions in factories all concerned the Lancashire cotton industry. The condition of the parish apprentices had been such as to give rise to the Health and Morals of Apprentices Act of 1802, introduced by Sir Robert Peel and designed to control the conditions of their employment. The first effective factory legislation was, however, the 1833 Factory Act which limited the hours worked by children and for the first time set up machinery for central inspection. A further Act of 1847, the Ten Hours Bill, extended protection to women and, with subsequent legislation, had the support of the landed gentry who saw it as a means of revenge against the manufacturers who had supported the repeal of the Corn Laws. In 1842 an Act was passed forbidding the employment of women and boys down the mines, but it was not until eight years later that the Coal Mines Act first listed coal mining as a 'Dangerous Trade'. With the amelioration of the conditions of the 'coalwhippers' in the London Docks, 1843 saw one of the few Acts regulating the employment of men. The Mercantile Marine Acts of 1850 and 1854 were passed to protect passengers and seamen, and match-making and other trades were declared dangerous by an Act of 1864.

Despite this and other legislation protecting the individual, the conditions of the employed working classes were generally very bad.

---

[1] Although overall living standards were raised throughout the century much poverty did in fact remain. See *Royal Commission on the Poor Law*.

[2] There were employers, among whom Robert Owen is perhaps the most well known, who were philanthropic in the extreme, providing education, insurance, pensions, and decent housing for their employees, but they were very much the exception.

It took years of agitation to get laws through Parliament; they were often concerned only with particular sectors of industry (the law was not extended to factories and workshops outside textiles until 1867) and they were often inadequately enforced for lack of the necessary administrative machinery.

The development of collective action

As a partial reaction to such conditions, but also because there was no legal regulation of wages, trades unions were bound to develop. This move to collective action, initially by skilled workers, was bitterly opposed by employers who felt it their duty not to bargain with organizations which they felt in any case to be outside the law, but to destroy them wherever possible. The law was obscure on the legal position of the unions, but in practice unionism suffered damaging reverses in the courts. Despite these difficulties the trades unions grew so that by the 1860s they represented a large proportion of skilled workers, more concerned with ensuring their share of the wealth provided by capitalism than with overthrowing the system. They were led by able men who could argue the case for the union movement persuasively. In 1868 the first trades union congress was held in Manchester. The previous year working men in towns had been given the vote. All this led to public debate, a Royal Commission and in 1871 the first of a series of Acts recognizing the rights of a union to exist on a par with employers and allowing union members to pursue such necessary action as picketing and protecting union funds.

Further collective action took place as consumers sought to protect themselves against the power of the manufacturers and retailers. The payment of wages in the form of goods, which were often of poor quality, had been declared illegal (the first Truck Act was passed in 1831), but there was much to be desired in the distribution, particularly, of food, where short measure and adulteration were the rule rather than the exception. It was not until 1860 that the Adulteration of Food Act gave limited power to local authorities to protect the consumer, and not until twelve years later that the first public analysts were appointed. The first tentative Weights and Measures legislation also had to wait until this time. Thus consumer co-operatives were founded, the first by the famous Rochdale Pioneers, and these received increasing State help as Acts were passed specifically to protect such exercises in mutual self-help, until in 1862 they were given corporate status with limited liability.

One of the most effective ways in which the State encouraged collective action was the granting of limited liability to any joint stock company that registered with the Board of Trade. The Acts of 1855 and 1862 led to a considerable increase in the development of companies now able to expand by using previously unavailable sources of finance.

The beginnings of State enterprise

Public enterprise began in 1861 with the establishment of the National Savings Bank under the control of the Post Office. In 1869 after an unsuccessful attempt to encourage provision by competition the inland telegraphs were nationalized, albeit at the expense of generous compensation to the railway and telegraph companies. This period also saw the beginnings of municipal enterprise as local authorities acquired or established companies to provide gas for domestic and industrial purposes.

Conclusion

Although there was a great liberalizing of economic activity, especially internationally, as the result of the acceptance of the doctrine of *laissez-faire*, it has been shown that the State continued to intervene in order to protect the individual, encourage some collective action, and even provide services itself. Protection of the individual not only reflected doubts, expressed by men such as Carlyle, Ruskin and, in his later years, J. S. Mill, as to the efficacy of individual freedom to provide 'the greatest happiness for the greatest numbers', but also the growing Christian Socialism which was working for the reform of a miserable and unjust society. Even so government expenditure was less than it might have been, with only the grosser abuses legislated against. The presence of the government was felt even less outside the social sphere as the rule of *laissez-faire* was felt to be responsible for the economic growth and world dominance that Britain experienced by the third quarter of the nineteenth century. But at least unquestioned adherence to the rule was no longer practised[1]; the way was open for the State intervention which took place with increasing regularity and extended motive and incidence from that time on.

---

[1] Theoretical acceptance of intervention with each case dealt with 'on its merits' is often associated with the economist W. S. Jevons who argued this in *The State in Relation to Labour* (1882). It should be noted that he restricted his approach to domestic policy, perhaps because there was less need for intervention in foreign trade at that time. See Eric Roll *History of Economic Thought*.

2.
1870–1914 TOWARDS INCREASING STATE ACTIVITY

External trade: demands for protection
It was in the period from 1870 to the outbreak of the 1914–18 War
that Britain began to lose her position as the dominant trading nation
of the world. This was the result of the emergence of industrialism,
originally in Germany, the United States and France, later in Sweden
and Russia and, after the turn of the century, in Canada and Japan.
It was the superior technology of Germany and the mass-production
techniques of the United States that industrialists most feared as they
pressed for a 'fair trade'[1] policy in response to the tariffs of Europe
and North America which were designed to protect their infant
industries. Further pressure advocated that there should be a special
relationship with the expanding Empire, trade with which was increasing at a relatively faster rate than with the rest of the world, and
in 1897 a return to Imperial Preference was announced which cut
across the arrangements previously made in Europe (see page 6).
The demands for protection were not confined to the industrialists;
the exploitation of the American Mid-West left the agricultural
industry in a sad state and led to a Royal Commission in 1882. But
for all the combined agitation, there was little positive action before
the 1914–18 War to protect an industrial structure based on an
established investment pattern. (It took time before the possibility of
a changed industrial structure was seen as an alternative or complement to protection.) This was mainly because world trade and in
particular Britain's trade with her colonies and China, was increasing
throughout the period and arguments for protection voiced in slumps[2]
were forgotten in the boom years, particularly from 1909–13.

---

[1] There were various voluntary associations established to press for
retaliation against foreign protection, the most famous being the
National Fair Trade League founded in 1881.

[2] It was in the Report of the Royal Commission on the Depression of
Trade and Industry published in 1887 that international competition was
first officially seen to be one of the factors most likely to affect future
industrial growth.

GOVERNMENT INTERVENTION AND INDUSTRIAL POLICY

Domestic developments

Towards collectivism

The trend to collective action continued, not least in the growth of the union movement which despite employer hostility and trade depression took place largely as the result of the development of industry-based unions of unskilled workers. By the end of the period the union movement was an accepted part of the country's social and industrial structure. Trade unionists were represented on official bodies, took an active part in local government and supported parliamentary candidates committed to the ideals of public ownership and control of the means of production. The Trades Disputes Act of 1906 and the Trade Union Act of 1913 had respectively removed the unions from the province of the law-courts[1] and allowed unions to use their funds for political purposes, provided the individual member had the right to contract out, both these pieces of legislation having reversed previous House of Lords judgements. With this recent legislation in its favour, a membership of over four million, experience of national strikes, the formation of the Triple Alliance (miners, railwaymen, and dockers committed to mutual support in the event of dispute with employers) and the growth of syndicalist ideas of workers' control, the union movement formed a powerful example of collectivist strength in the years immediately preceding the 1914–18 War.

A necessary complement to the growth of unions was the development of permanent Employers' Associations. At the same time Trade Associations representing particular industries or areas (Chambers of Commerce) grew in number as employers desired joint action as a protection against foreign competition which was benefiting from the trusts and cartels which had developed relatively early in the industrialization of the United States and Germany. There was also an increase in the number of professional and technical associations.[2]

The development of collective representation on both sides of industry not only facilitated the bargaining process, increasingly seen as an acceptable means of obtaining agreement, but also gave the State the opportunity to recognize and in some cases reduce in-

---

[1] This unique privilege was held by the unions until the introduction of the 1971 Industrial Relations Act. The present obstructive attitude of the T.U.C. is just one indication that a policy of 'legal enforcement' might be very difficult to implement in the field of industrial relations.

[2] For details of these see J. W. Grove, *Government and Industry in Britain*, Chapter 1.

dustrial strife. This it did under the 1896 Conciliation Act following the Royal Commission on Labour (1889–92).

Increasing public enterprise

The increase in municipal enterprise was given impetus by the reform of local government between 1882 and 1894. Even so this only applied to 'genuine' public utilities where the efficiency of the single unit was obvious, and municipal ownership was the easiest way of avoiding consumer exploitation. The extension of municipal enterprise, which in the minds of the Webbs and other Fabians would have led to State Socialism, did not in fact appeal to working-class movements and in practice was seldom attempted by local authorities. In the event, apart from the obvious octopoid industries such as gas and water, local transport services and airports, and the provision of social capital, including council housing, the local authorities have been remarkably reluctant to extend their activity.

Despite the acceptance of collective action and State intervention in many spheres, the continuing strength of the *laissez-faire* doctrine of competition can be judged from the history of the development of the telephone service. In defiance of a High Court ruling that the telephone came under the Telegraph Acts and as such was the responsibility of the Postmaster General, private telephone companies developed the service under licence from the government which was itself to provide the trunk service. In 1884, however, the companies were allowed to construct their own trunk lines and, not surprisingly, by 1890 this had led to a near monopoly by one company, the National Telephone Company. The Government then tried a system of market division between the National Telephone Company and the Post Office, and subsequently competition between these two and municipal enterprises, before finally and belatedly nationalizing the system in 1912.

Working conditions legislation

The development of the unions and their power to ameliorate conditions of work by no means extended to all workers. Thus there was still need for legislation to protect some workers and improve the lot of others. In 1891 the House of Commons adopted the 'Fair Wages Resolution' which required all government contractors to pay wage rates commensurate with those paid by other firms in the same district. This resolution, which ensured that the contractor did not cut wage rates in order to lower his tender, was soon adopted by the local

13

authorities. Owing to the dispersed and small size of individual out-
lets, retailing was an industry in which unions had not developed.
Thus various Shop Acts were passed regulating hours (1892, 1895),
the provision of seats (1899), and weekly half-day holidays (1911).
Acts were also passed limiting the number of hours worked: in 1893
the Board of Trade was given the power to deal with excessive over-
time on railways and in 1908 there followed the Coal Mines (Eight
Hours) Act. Legislation in 1891 and 1895 had not only extended the
number and type of workplaces subject to regulation, but had brought
the local authorities to the aid of the expanding factory inspectorate.
The Factory Workshop Act of 1901 was a piece of tidying legislation.
Laundries were belatedly included in an Act of 1907. Increased protection was given to children by the Employment of Children Act of
1903, which prohibited their employment if it endangered their
physical health or adversely affected their education. Merchant
seamen received their own special protection under legislation passed
in 1894 and 1906.

The Workmen's Compensation Act of 1897 introduced the
principle of employer liability for the insurance of workers against
industrial injury, but there was still much abuse of working people,
particularly women, in the so called 'sweated trades'. Evil conditions
and minimal payment in many small workshops led to the Trade
Boards Act of 1909 which fixed minimum wages in such trades as
chain making, lace making, and tailoring. A further interference in
the labour market was the Minimum Wage Act, which in 1912
brought to an end a national strike of coalminers who had long
complained that to vary wages with the price of coal was iniquitous.

Social legislation
Government interference in the form of social legislation had continued with the Public Health Act of 1848. The concentration of
primitive sanitary conditions brought to the rapidly expanding towns
from rural areas meant ill-health and death for many, especially in the
poorer districts. Added to this were the sporadic outbreaks of cholera
and typhus which eventually led to the Report on Sanitary Conditions
of the Labouring Population in 1842. This report, primarily the work
of Edwin Chadwick, argued that the high death rate stemmed
directly from bad sanitation and that this could be avoided by public
action. The Act laid down common standards and gave local authorities the responsibility of meeting them, under the supervision of the
centralized General Board of Health. In fact less was done than might

have been[1] and it was not until the Public Health Act of 1875 that a modern public health system began, and even then there was no centrally responsible authority until the Ministry of Health was established in 1918.

A further source of agitation for reformers such as Octavia Hill was the low standard of housing to be found in the towns. The Government was very slow to recognize its responsibility here. The common lodging house came under regulation in 1851, but it was not until the Acts of 1866 and 1875 that local authorities were empowered to order private landlords to correct insanitary conditions and condemn, demolish and reconstruct slum properties. The idea of the town as a place in which to live a full life, with parks, libraries and other amenities provided by the local authority, was slow to materialize, although the lack of such municipal provision was in part due to the inadequate machinery of local government before its reform in the 1880s. Only 15,000 houses were provided by local authorities before 1914, although many more were rendered fit for human habitation, especially after the Housing and Town Planning Act of 1909. There was, therefore, much scope for the private trusts which provided numerous blocks of working-class tenements in places like London's East End.

The provision of a national system of free compulsory education followed naturally on from Factory Acts and Poor Law legislation, which required that children covered by the law in this way should receive some sort of rudimentary education. Further it was realized that there was a need for technical literacy as industry progressed and foreign competition increased. It was not, however, until 1870 that the first Education Act was passed which provided free primary education, the delaying factor this time being the struggle between the established and nonconformist church, both of which provided voluntary education and neither of which wished to see the other better favoured by the law, rather than the argument that compulsory education was an infringement of individual liberty. Further Acts in 1876, 1880 and 1891 extended education to the elementary level. The first provision of secondary education was made in an Act passed in

---

[1] The principle of individual freedom is well illustrated here in a comment from *The Times* quoted by J. B. Brebner, '*Laissez-faire* and State intervention in nineteenth-century Britain', *Essays in Economic History*, volume 3, Ed. E. M. Carus-Wilson: 'We prefer to take our chance of cholera and the rest, than to be bullied into health.'

1902, and soon after this local authorities were authorized to provide meals and compelled to appoint School Medical Officers.

Social legislation received perhaps its greatest impetus from a change in the attitude to the poor. Contrasting with the mid-Victorian optimism concerning living standards and increased material well-being expressed by men like Sir Robert Giffen, came the results of empirical studies undertaken in the poorer sections of large cities. For the first time poverty was quantified and the complacency of the optimists was shattered. Conditions had been described before, see for example Henry Mayhew, *London Labour and the London Poor* (1862), but a greater impact was made by the 'reality' of the statistics. The studies by men such as Charles Booth[1] and Seebohm Rowntree[2] showed that 10 per cent of the urban population of London, York and other cities lived in a perpetual state of need, while a further 20 per cent lived below a fairly low poverty line.

With the formation of County Councils and County Boroughs the administration of poor relief had become more effective, but need for rationalization coupled with the trade depression of 1902–4 led to the Royal Commission on the Poor Law which sat from 1905–9. Unfortunately, if inevitably, composed as it was of existing Poor Law administrators, but also people such as Booth, Beatrice Webb and representatives of the working class such as George Lansbury, the Commission produced both a majority and minority report. They agreed on such things as the acceptance of the County and County Borough as the administrative units, the abolition of the mixed workhouse, the desire to change the view that the acceptance of relief inevitably meant the loss of self-dignity, and the need for the provision of employment exchanges and public works to alleviate the miseries of unemployment; they divided on the cause of poverty, with the minority report, primarily the work of Beatrice Webb, reflecting the view, still not acceptable to some, that poverty resulted from the social conditions in which the poor found themselves, not from any lack of moral fibre on their part. The Commission's recommendations suggested a system of welfare in the form of, for example, education, pensions and medical services, which would provide the individual with a minimum standard of living, below which he should not be allowed to drop; and this contrasted violently with the concept of individual freedom which still had many supporters.

---

[1] *Life and Labour of the People in London.*
[2] *Poverty; a Study of Town Life.*

In the event the rationalization and extension of social welfare did not take place in any comprehensive sense, but a series of *ad hoc* Acts passed before the 1914–18 War showed the increasing rate of growth of State intervention. These Acts included the Pensions Act of 1908, a pension being the alternative to the workhouse for the old, whom Booth had found to be disproportionately in need of poor relief, an Act of 1909 authorizing the Board of Trade to establish local labour exchanges,[1] the first of which opened a year later, and the National Insurance Act of 1911, providing both unemployment and sickness benefit at that time for selected groups of workers. Obviously the legislation concerned with minimum hours of work and rates of pay (see page 14) can also be considered here, reflecting as it did the desirability of a national minimum standard of living.

Extension of motive for State intervention
In 1900, as a reaction to the technological advance and military pretensions of Germany, the National Physical Laboratory was established. Prestige was the motive for a £2½m. government loan to the Cunard Company which made possible the building of the *Lusitania* and *Mauritania*. And the strategic consideration of ensuring the Navy's oil supplies in the event of war led to the Government securing a controlling interest in the Anglo-Persian Oil Company in 1913.

Conclusion
By 1914 the *laissez-faire* philosophy was no longer considered sufficient in theory nor necessary in practice. This is illustrated by the pressure for protection and special relationships in international transactions voiced by the less secure manufacturers, and domestically by the development of collective action on both sides of industry, the beginnings of municipal and State enterprise, increased social legislation of all kinds, and the introduction of positive measures to support industry for a variety of reasons.

---

[1] The case for labour exchanges was forcibly argued by W. H. Beveridge (later Lord Beveridge). See his *Unemployment; A Problem of Industry*, published in 1909 which recognized for the first time the diversity of causes of unemployment, and argued that a policy attacking the root causes would do much to relieve the destitution and poverty that was still considered by many to be unavoidable. He was in fact one of the civil servants instrumental in getting the Labour Exchanges Act on the statute books.

Further, with the exploitation of the joint stock principle and rationalization of commercial legislation,[1] individual enterprises were increasing in size so that much of the country's prosperity depended less on the individual entrepreneur. With increased size came the opportunity to exploit monopolistic and quasi-monopolistic situations and therefore the need for government recognition and control. There was little done by the Government in this field before the 1914–18 War, especially compared with the active role taken by governments in the United States and Germany, but an exception was the Railway and Canal Traffic Act of 1894 which sought to regulate rates and obviate discrimination in an industry where the Government's approach had needed to change from one of fostering competition to one of controlling amalgamation.

The level and structure of taxation can be taken as a barometer of these changing attitudes. Increased government expenditure had meant that government gross income had increased threefold from 1870–1914. Further there had been a movement towards a relatively more progressive system of taxation in the twenty years before the 1914–18 War. In 1894 death duties had been both increased and graduated; in 1907 a distinction was made between earned and unearned income, with higher rates for the latter; two years later super-tax was introduced; and in the last Budget before the war income tax, super-tax and death duties were all increased. This meant that while revenue from customs and excise duties had not even doubled between 1870 and the war, there had been a four-fold increase in property and income tax, while death duties had increased five times.[2] A large proportion of total government income still came from custom and excise duties, however, and the working man continued to contribute more on average than he received in benefit right up to 1914. The increase in government activity, mainly for social, but also now for strategic and other reasons, was still relatively unambitious, as is illustrated by the further statistic that between the wars government expenditure never fell below four times the 1914 level. There still had to be a very good reason for intervention before the Government took action. But views were changing, both as the result of pressure of circumstance, as with the demands for protection, and also following more detailed study of the social structure, as with the change in

---

[1] For example Trade Marks Act 1875, Bankruptcy Act 1883, Patents Act 1883.

[2] Mitchell and Deane, *Abstract of British Historical Statistics*.

attitude towards the poor. It is obvious, therefore, that the Government would have extended its activity even had the war not accelerated the process. The fact that the Government took few immediate steps to control the economy at the outbreak of war, however, indicates the residual strength of the rule of *laissez-faire*. Intervention was reserved for the exceptional circumstance, and the war did not initially fall into this category.

3.
1914–1918 THE EFFECTS OF THE WAR

'Business as usual'
Apart from a short financial crisis in July, the outbreak of war made little initial impact on the economy. It was felt that the market economy would automatically reallocate resources in answer to any change in government expenditure favouring strategic requirements, and that in any case, since the war would last only a few months at the outside, there was no need for the clutter of government control. However, the railways were requisitioned, some exports were controlled, and the Government entered the market to buy wheat in bulk and control sugar supplies now that beet sugar was no longer available from the continent. With the rejection of a proposal to requisition the larger munitions factories in October 1914, the Government's approach was clearly indicated. The war was to be run under private enterprise; it was to be 'business as usual'. The war did, however, produce one of the earliest examples of direct State assistance to a particular industry. Up to the outbreak of war Britain had been importing 90 per cent of her dyestuffs from Germany and, naturally, it was not long before the textile industry was faced with a shortage of dyes. The Government was therefore instrumental in the formation of a new company, British Dyes Ltd, with much of the original capital supplied by the Treasury. At the end of the war the company was amalgamated with the largest private concern in the industry, Levinstein Ltd, to form the British Dyestuffs Corporation.[1]

Introduction of control
By 1916 it was obvious not only that the war was going to last, but also that private enterprise was not coping with the situation. The shortage of munitions, a pattern of recruitment which took little notice of the needs of the economy as it accepted those who were prepared to fight, but who would have better served their country by

---

[1] The Government at this stage had the right to appoint two directors to the Board and regulate prices but sold its right when the company became part of the newly established I.C.I. in 1926 (see page 30).

staying in essential employment, and short supply leading to price increases coupled with the ability by some to make enormous sums by profiteering; all these led to public opinion accepting the tight hold which Lloyd George was to place on the economy when he came to power in December of that year.

The control of productive capacity was both detailed and wide ranging and included the acquisition of the coal industry, flour-mills, iron-mines and canals; the requisitioning of factories to make arms; the bulk buying of food and raw materials; various controls on industrial production and international and domestic trade; price-fixing and rationing; direction of merchant shipping, shipbuilding, docks and harbours; and control of farming, including guaranteed prices and a minimum wage for labourers under the Corn Production Act of 1917.

The Government also intervened to fix wages. In February 1915 a Committee on production in engineering and shipbuilding establishments had been set up in order to cope with any problems the war was creating. The most urgent problem concerned labour relations and so the Committee found itself fixing wages. After the Munitions of War Act of July 1915 made its decisions binding, the Committee extended its coverage to other industries which, though not subject to the Act, accepted regulation in the peculiar circumstances of war. The Committee extended its work to deal with questions of dilution of labour which greatly concerned the unions. Further interference in the labour market took the form of various Military Service Acts, the development of a system of reserved occupations and tentative efforts, in the event unsuccessful, to outlaw strikes.

Institutional changes

Such control obviously involved much contact between civil servants, businessmen and trade unionists and barriers were broken down as a result. The position of the unions was one of increasing power and prestige, with several trade unionists holding Ministerial office during the war.

The mechanics of control involved the development of trade associations as representatives of industry, and the war saw the formation of three national bodies representing large groups of employers; in 1915 the National Union of Manufacturers (originally the Association of British Manufacturers and more recently the National Association of British Manufacturers), in 1916, the Federation of British Industry, and in 1919, the British Employers Confederation, concerned with industrial relations.[1]

Government intervention and control had finally been deemed necessary in the special wartime situation, but once the war was over individual control was quickly restored to the private sector and most of the consultative machinery was abolished. The war, however, had shown various advantages to State intervention and precedents had been created, so that the country never fully returned to the pre-war degree of economic freedom.

---

[1] The three leading employers associations merged to form the Confederation of British Industry on 1st August 1965. This was done primarily in order to present a united front, particularly at the N.E.D.C., see page 56.

4.
1919–1939 WORLD DEPRESSION AND INCREASED GOVERNMENT INTERVENTION

A characteristic of industrial capitalism had been the cyclical nature of economic activity: boom periods of relatively high rates of activity, investment, level of employment, prices and wages, followed by the reciprocal slump situation.[1] A comprehensive assessment of the causes of the trade cycle is beyond the scope of this book; what is important here is the examination of the changes in government industrial policy brought about by the increased intensity and duration of the slump years in a country which no longer dominated world trade and finance.

Britain emerged from the war in a much weaker position; capital was run down, export markets were lost, some irrevocably, and the industrial structure was in any case distorted by the fact that staple industries had been expanded in the war when in normal circumstances the pressures of comparative advantage would have hastened their decline. After an initial restocking boom there began in 1920 a two-year slump. This was followed by a period of depression throughout the twenties and thirties heightened by the world economic crisis of 1929–33. The slow recovery after this, culminating in the re-armament boom from 1937–9, came too late to keep trade free, as by then there had developed a complexity of protection, preference and bilateral agreement with the Government desperately seeking to defend domestic industry and provide employment.

In pre-war times the trade cycle had been accepted as a fact of capitalist life, although there was for the first time some resistance to

---

[1] The slumps of the late 1870s, 1885–6, which led to the Royal Commission on the Depression of Trade, and 1903–4, which led to the Royal Commission on the Poor Law, have already been mentioned. There were two other periods of relative inactivity in the years preceding the war; 1890–5 and 1908.

wage cutting in the 1908 slump. Industry had its inactive periods but it always recovered and the underlying secular movement had throughout been one of growth. But in the twenties and thirties industry did not recover. The initial post-war restocking boom was doomed to be short-lived. When the boom broke in the summer of 1920 it was primarily export led; the world too had restocked. Unfortunately this restocking process had meant the continued production at pre-war, and in some cases war expanded, levels in the staple industries. For these there was to be much less subsequent demand, as foreign competition increased[1] in world markets which were in any case not going to remain stable. It was unemployment in these industries and the areas in which these industries had originally settled, for example Lancashire, South Wales, the North-East and Scotland, which was primarily responsible for a hard core of over a million men idle throughout the period, and which accelerated the rate of acceptance of State intervention.[2] The unemployment percentage was never below 10 per cent throughout the whole of the inter-war period and in 1932, the worst year, two and three-quarter million people were registered as unemployed. This represented 22·5 per cent of the working population. Percentages of insured workers unemployed in particular industries in that year illustrate the disproportionate incidence of unemployment. In coalmining the figure was 35 per cent; iron and steel, 45 per cent; cotton textiles, 30 per cent (it had been 43 per cent the year before); and shipbuilding 62 per cent.[3]

The move to protection

The official response to unemployment levels of this order was to heed the industrialists' calls for protection. The reintroduction of non-revenue duties had begun in the war. In 1915, as a wartime measure to restrict the use of shipping, discourage expenditure on luxuries and

---

[1] This was accentuated by a return to the Gold Standard at pre-war parity in 1925. The pound was overvalued at this rate and many exports were priced out of world markets.

[2] Much has been written on the suffering of the unemployed in the 1930s, the reading of which would give those who cannot remember those times an insight into the working of the mind of the older unionist who is so often condemned outright for a restrictive attitude. See for example *Men Without Work*, A Report to the Pilgrim Trust 1938.

[3] For further details see Mitchell and Deane, *Abstract of Historical Statistics*.

conserve foreign exchange, the McKenna duties were imposed on, for example, motor-cars, motor-cycles and their accessories, and musical instruments. The first admission of protection came with the retention of these duties throughout the inter-war period, apart from a short period in 1924 when they were abolished by the minority Labour Government. In 1920 the Dyestuffs Import Regulation Act prohibited the import of dyestuffs, except under licence from the Board of Trade, as the Government continued to support an industry in which it had direct interest. The following year saw the Safeguarding of Industries Act which placed a $33\frac{1}{3}$ per cent *ad valorem* duty on competitive imports of certain strategic industries. Five years later the duty was extended to cover non-strategic goods and in some cases the duty was increased to 50 per cent. The original Act had also placed an *ad valorem* duty on goods which were being 'dumped' in this country. The Finance Act of 1925 gave assistance to the British rayon industry by imposing duties on various imported competitive products, and the British film industry was considerably stimulated by the Cinematograph Film Act which placed a quota on foreign films.

Free trade was finally and universally abandoned after the world monetary crisis of 1931, which had led to the abolition of the gold standard. With unemployment levels never having been so high, the MacDonald National Government had been returned with an enormous protectionist majority and in February 1932 the Import Duties Act, which placed a general 10 per cent tariff on most imported goods, was the inevitable result. The exceptions mainly concerned trade with the dominions and colonies, and this Imperial Preference was extended after the Ottawa Conference which took place in the summer of the same year. The general feature of the years before the war, however, was one of increased protection in the form of additional tariffs, supplemented on occasions by import quotas.

Direct support to industry
In addition to this general protective policy the Government began to support those sectors of industry which for various reasons found themselves unsuited to the world economic climate of the period. Industries were encouraged to rationalize, that is amalgamate, restrict entry, fix prices and reduce productive capacity, for in this way, it was hoped, competitive waste would be reduced, inefficient firms eliminated and the resulting structure would make them better able

25

to withstand the pressures of world competition.[1] Actual support took many forms but mostly involved the Government providing money in the form of subsidies or loans. A wide range of industries was involved from the old staple industries such as coal and cotton to newly developed industries like beet sugar and civil aviation. In some cases industries took the initiative themselves, in others there was need for coercion and enforcement.

The Trade Facilities Acts of 1921–6 were general in their application, providing as they did Treasury guarantees for loans made from private sources. Other measures were more specific and when introduced were not always graciously received by employers, who not only disliked the bureaucratic interference of government but also feared, in some cases with reason, that such help was merely an intermediate step in the direction of State ownership.

Coal
This last point is illustrated by the lack of success the Government had in changing the structure of the coal industry. The Government had taken control of the mines in the war, but not until 1917. Little had been done, therefore, to reorganize an industry comprising too many small and uneconomic units before it was returned to private ownership after the Sankey Commission had failed to agree on the question of nationalization in 1919. The newly created Mines Department met with little success in fostering rationalization. In an industry where labour relations were bad, productivity was falling and demand for exports was even further reduced by a return to the gold standard at pre-war parity in 1926, it is not surprising that a toothless Mining Industry Act of 1926, following two Courts of Inquiry and a Royal Commission under the chairmanship of Lord Samuel, achieved little more success. By 1930, with the industry near financial collapse, the Government was forced to introduce legislation, creating a Coal Mines Reorganization Commission which had the power to enforce amalgamation and promote the rational marketing of coal. At the same time the industry was given the right to fix prices and regulate output. Employer antagonism and House of Lords amendments again limited the power of the Commission. An attempt was made to

---

[1] The Government's case was summed up in the 1929 Balfour Committee Report on Industry and Trade which specifically argued for enlargement and regrouping of industrial units as a prerequisite for recovery.

strengthen it in 1936. The Coal Act of 1938, which also nationalized the coal measures, replaced it with the new Coal Commission, but the record of amalgamation and rationalization brought about by government persuasion remained a dismal one up to the outbreak of war.

Railways

In most industries the Government was slow to intervene. Railways were an exception. Under the Railways Act of 1921 the railway companies were organized into four regional undertakings which could if required pool resources. In 1914 there had been one hundred and twenty private companies, so many in fact that for efficient war-time distribution the system had been centrally controlled. Even so the subsequent reorganization under the Act was a remarkable piece of rationalization.

Cotton

In the cotton industry *ad hoc* private attempts to reduce surplus capacity and introduce short-time working culminated in 1929 in the creation of the Lancashire Cotton Corporation Ltd. This was an amalgamation of over two hundred mills supported financially by the Bank of England, which intended to improve the better mills and scrap the rest, in an effort to reduce spindle capacity. Progress was slow even after the establishment of a Spindles Board by Act of Parliament in 1936. The industry was individualistic and there was jealousy between the various sections, so that it was continued trade depression that eventually brought into being the joint Committee of Cotton Trade Organizations representing the industry as a whole and largely responsible for the Cotton Industry (Reorganization) Act of 1939. Under this Act surplus capacity and excess competition were to be eliminated but before it could be put into effect the war had begun.

Iron and Steel

It was not until 1932 that the Government took a hand in the iron and steel industry. A $33\frac{1}{3}$ per cent tariff was placed on iron and steel imports on the condition that the industry rationalized and thus improved efficiency. The co-ordinating body was to be the British Iron and Steel Federation set up in 1934, the year in which the protective tariff was raised to 50 per cent. The Federation became one of the strongest trade associations in the country, more concerned, however, with promoting restrictive practices both at home and abroad than with establishing a more efficient structure.

Shipbuilding
In the shipbuilding industry, which faced intense competition from abroad throughout the inter-war period, there was little reaction to an early government report urging reorganization until 1930, when the Shipbuilding Conference formed the National Shipbuilders' Security Ltd with money provided by the Bankers' Industrial Development Company Ltd. Its purpose was to buy up and scrap obsolete yards, selling the sites for non-shipbuilding purposes. In the event the industry was contracted by about one third in the nine years up to the war, but a policy of restricting competition and fixing prices more than counteracted the beneficial effects of the rationalization process.

Agriculture
The Agricultural Marketing Acts of 1931 and 1933 made provision for producers to control the marketing of any agricultural product. Provided the Government approved, any such scheme could come into operation. It involved all the producers in the industry, including those who had not agreed to the scheme, and was run by a Board elected by the producers themselves. Boards were established for hops (1932) and milk (for England and Wales and three areas in Scotland in 1933 and 1934). A regulatory Board[1] was established for potatoes in 1933.

The shortage of sugar in the war led the Government to encourage the production of sugar beet under the British Sugar (Subsidy) Act of 1925. The subsidy was to decline once the industry was established, but the unlikely chance of this happening was finally lost when world sugar prices collapsed in 1929–32. The industry, a perfect example of an 'infant industry' unable to grow up and stand on its own feet, continued to require government support, which it was given under the Sugar Industry (Reorganization) Act in 1936. By this time much of agriculture was in any case receiving direct subsidy. After the abortive Agriculture Act of 1920, which had replaced the 1917 Corn Production Act with guaranteed prices that were impossible to finance after the collapse of world prices, and which had therefore been

---

[1] There are two types of Marketing Board. In addition to market regulation the Trading Board actually buys and sells the product.

repealed within the year, little had been done until the further collapse in the price of agricultural goods on world markets between 1929 and 1932. After this, however, meat was protected by arrangements made at the Ottawa Conference, wheat was supported by the Wheat Act of 1932 which guaranteed a standard price, livestock was eventually given permanent help under the 1937 Livestock Industry Act, and by the end of the thirties only potatoes were not receiving subsidy and the National Farmers Union had prepared a system of guaranteed prices which was to serve as the basis of post-war policy. The fishing industry was also in receipt of government assistance through the Herring Industry Board (1935) and the White Fish Commission (1938).

Civil Aviation
The civil aviation industry first received a subsidy in 1921. This was used primarily for internal competition between the companies as they struggled to keep in the European market against State-subsidized foreign rivals. A further subsidy was granted in 1922 on the condition that some sort of rationalization of routes should take place. When this failed, the Hambling Committee recommended compulsory amalgamation into a single unit and the Imperial Air Transport Company (later Imperial Airways) was formed. This company secured a near monopoly position, in the main due to the receipt of government subsidy, but neglect of European routes led to the formation of another subsidized company, British Airways, out of existing unsubsidized companies. In 1939 the two companies were combined to become the publicly owned British Overseas Airways Corporation.

The right to intervene
With these and other measures[1] it can be seen that the Government was prepared to encourage, coerce and at times enforce rationalization of the structure of much of the country's industry in order to make it more specific to the economy's needs. As has been illustrated, the degree to which the Government was successful in bringing about all aspects of rationalization varied with such things as the conditions within the industry, the pressure of overseas competition, the movement of world prices and the behaviour of industrialists who on

---

[1] For example, Cunard were again given government assistance, this time to build the sister ships, *Queen Mary* and *Queen Elizabeth*.

balance were probably keener to accept the subsidies, restrict competition, and fix prices, than to reduce capacity.

What is certain, however, is that the period between the wars saw the final, if in some cases reluctant, acceptance of the need for State support for industry. Free trade had given way to protection; a large proportion of industry, particularly the long-established and declining sector, was receiving government assistance in one way or another, and there had been further examples of direct State organization and control. B.O.A.C. has already been mentioned. There were also the Forestry Commission, established in 1919 to replenish the war-depleted stock of timber, and in 1926 the Central Electricity Board, the first of the modern public corporations. The British Broadcasting Corporation received a Royal Charter a year later and in 1933 the London Passenger Transport Board was established to provide an integrated transport service for Greater London.

Concentration of private industry

The recognition of the need to rationalize, involving the acceptance of amalgamation and mutual trading policies, meant the rejection of the principle of free competition which had been supported so forcibly as the best means of resource allocation by the supporters of *laissez-faire.* It was not only under government stimulus that concentration took place. Moves to monopolistic and oligopolistic structure occurred in several industries as businessmen came to realize that perhaps the depression in trade was not as temporary as they had thought, and also that the larger, more centralized units in the United States and Germany were better able to cope with the situation anyway. Thus amalgamation took place in, for example, specialized engineering trades, in the match industry and in the production of whisky and industrial alcohol (Distillers Company 1927). The most important merger was the formation of I.C.I. in 1926. Four firms were involved: Nobel Industries Ltd, Brunner, Mond and Co. Ltd, United Alkali Co. Ltd, and the British Dyestuffs Corporation Ltd.

At the same time technological advances were taking place which required increases in the size of the business unit to achieve reductions in unit costs. An obvious example of this was the introduction of mass production methods in the motor-car industry. As a result the number of firms in the industry in 1939 was one-third of the 1918 figure and by then the six largest producers were responsible for 90 per cent of total output.

Assessment of government policy

Although the Government was taking positive steps to assist industry, given the economic position its overall economic policy was designed if anything to aggravate the situation. This was mainly because the economic theory of the twenties and early thirties was not sufficiently developed to cope with the situation, and orthodox policies of balancing the Budget and reducing government expenditure meant that demand, and therefore employment opportunities, were reduced rather than increased. When the breakthrough did come in the *General Theory* of J. M. Keynes in 1936, so radical were its proposals that it was bound to take time to be accepted by the policy-makers, who in any case did not have the machinery available for the collection and analysis of data that the application of Keynes' ideas required. Support for those who argued with Keynes for greater public expenditure came in the form of successes achieved in reducing unemployment in the centrally controlled states of Russia, on the one hand, and Germany and Italy on the other, although whether such results could be achieved within a democracy was questioned at the time. The *ad hoc* measures of government expenditure and support in the United States, the 'New Deal', did not give conclusive proof that it could.

The revival, when it did come, owed less to the Government than to the fact that while the older established industries and areas were declining, the new industries, centred in the Midlands and the South East were expanding to meet the demands of the four out of five workers who *were* employed and whose discretionary income was increasing both as the result of higher incomes and, after 1927, the fall in imported food prices. The industries most responsible were housing, consumer durables, electricity and related industries including radio, motors, and chemicals.

As activity increased in the Midlands and the South East so did the demand for housing, and this was intensified in the thirties by the low rate of interest introduced by the authorities in the crisis of 1931. Thus with improvements in transport the thirties saw the development of vast areas of sprawling suburbia and ribbon development which, however displeasing to the eye, at least provided work not only for those directly concerned but for those in the industries supplying raw materials and providing furniture, consumer durables and other goods with which the homes were equipped. This secondary demand was partially responsible for revival in some of the older industries. The steel industry, for example, benefited from the expansion of the motor industry. Here the protection afforded since 1932 was instrumental in ensuring that such raw materials were provided by domestic suppliers. Finally, of course, the rearmament programme added its share to the demands of industry, particularly heavy industry, including the rapidly expanding manufacture of aircraft.

Conclusion

The inter-war period was primarily one of depression and mass regional unemployment. The Government was thus forced to go to the assistance of the economy as it was increasingly recognized that market forces and free competition both at home and in world markets were not enough to ensure the full use of the country's existing capacity, the structure of which was in any case inappropriate to the post-war situation. The Government's overall policy, based on misconceptions as to the working of the economy, did little to help the situation, and the assistance given to industry in the form of protection from foreign competition and encouragement to rationalization was really a case of attacking the symptoms rather than the disease. But by the end of the period the Government had not only experienced much closer contact with industry, but also become aware of the increasing demands for some sort of economic planning and the development of an economic theory which would provide the means to such an end. In the event the tight government controls of the 1939–45 War served to accelerate the movement towards active government participation and the development of the mixed economy.

5.
1939–1945 THE EFFECT OF THE WAR

Immediate government control

As might be expected, there was no question in 1939 that the war might be run by private enterprise; it was accepted automatically that the Government's responsibility was to allocate resources and regulate the forces of the market. Controls were introduced immediately, initially dealing with imports, foreign exchange and the use of materials, but eventually covering all aspects of the economy. The industrialist virtually surrendered his entrepreneurial function as his sources of finance, raw materials from home or abroad, the destination of an often government-specified finished article, its price, the profit he could receive and distribute to his shareholders and the site and location of his factory, were all subject to licence, registration, approval or some other form of government direction or control. In some industries the Government followed a policy whereby production was limited to a given number of firms, who themselves compensated the rest of the firms in the industry who were forced to close down. The control of agriculture was of necessity extremely strict; in the final event a farmer could be evicted if his standards fell below those prescribed.

The worker too was imprisoned in a complex of control, as to the type of his employment, the hours and conditions of work entailed, his right to leave such employment and move to another position or area and his right to strike, which he was officially unable to do. And everyone, as a consumer, was subject to the rationing of essentials and the non-existence or tax-inflated price of many luxuries. The introduction of purchase tax in 1940 restricting consumption, and therefore production of less essentials, and providing the Government with revenue from remaining purchases, is an example of the way in which the Government manipulated consumption to serve the needs of the war economy. The control of consumption in any case took on a new importance as Keynesian arguments for the regulation of aggregate demand as a means of effective overall control of the economy were at last accepted by the Government. From 1941 control of private consumption for this purpose was complemented by the abandonment of the orthodox measure of balancing the Budget, and a policy of deficit and surplus financing was introduced as a means of adjusting the Government's contribution to total demand.

Although controls were introduced immediately, the fact that intervention had been piecemeal, and by no means comprehensive in the thirties, meant that it took some three years for the country to be completely mobilized.[1] By the end of the war, however, not only had the slack been taken up but so great was the central control that four out of five people in the manufacturing industry were directly or indirectly engaged in work for the Government.

Further stimulus to collective action

The mechanics of control gave further impetus to the collectivization process. The trade associations acted as government agents in the administration of regulation and control and in many cases provided the personnel to supplement the civil servants on controlling bodies. Their growth was further encouraged by the need, under the 1940 Conditions of Employment Order, to ensure that wages and conditions in an industry did not fall below agreed levels. The unions having lost favour in the inter-war period, both with their members and with the Government, were revitalized by the war. This was caused, in the first instance, by full employment which strengthened their bargaining power, and in the second by the fact that they were accepted as equals both by organized industry and the Government. Co-operation of the workers was deemed essential in this time of crisis. With union membership at more than nine million in 1945 and Ernest Bevin as Minister of Labour in the War Cabinet, the unions had begun an era of unprecedented power and authority.

Government departments

The administration of controls also gave rise to new government departments, and changes in the names and functions of others. Some of these departments were to be wartime expedients only, but others were to remain. Thus, for example, 1939 saw the creation of the Ministry of Supply and the Ministry of Economic Warfare, and 1942 the Ministry of Production. Of these the Ministry of Supply was the only one to survive the war, being merged with the Ministry of Aircraft Production. The existing Department of Mines became the

---

[1] This is extremely well illustrated by the figures for Total Registered Unemployed in Great Britain which were in 1939, 1,514,000; 1940, 963,000; 1941, 350,000; and 1942, 123,000. See Mitchell and Deane.

Ministry of Fuel and Power and this was to remain after the war along with the war-created Ministry of Food.

Responsibility for planning in peace
The controls of the war left a permanent mark on the relationship between the Government and industry. The most important was the Government's acceptance of its responsibility for overall planning in peace as well as in war. This policy, reflecting the views of men like Keynes and Beveridge, was expressed in the White Paper *Employment Policy After the War* published in 1944. The objectives of the Government as planner can be summarized by: (*a*) maintenance of a high and stable level of employment, (*b*) stability of the internal purchasing power of money, (*c*) economic growth and an increased standard of living, and (*d*) protection of the external situation by ensuring that such policies did not upset the balance of payments situation. Postwar history was to tell how far these mutually conflicting policies were pursued successfully or not by successive governments, all of which accepted the White Paper but which gave different weights to the various objectives according to external pressure or political leaning.[1] As a blue print for control within the framework of the private ownership of capital, however, the White Paper was an historic document.

Conclusion
The problems facing the Government at the end of the war were unprecedented in degree. Export markets had contracted, capital equipment was run down, foreign assets had been sold to pay for the war, heavy debts had been incurred overseas and problems like the dichotomy between the active and inactive areas were bound to recur. There were, however, some grounds for the optimism which always follows the holocaust. The principle of economic planing had been accepted, a blueprint prepared. The experience and machinery of control were readily available. Contacts and co-operation had been established between the Government, organized industry and the unions. Economists and statisticians were increasingly employed in government departments and this led to an improvement in analytical techniques which accelerated their acceptance by established civil servants. And finally, the economic theory, for all the academic argument and subsequent refinement, had been developed to provide the planner with the basic tools of his trade.

---

[1] See *The Control of the Economy* by D. Lee in this series.

6.
1945–1950 RECOVERY THROUGH CONTROL

The Government's responsibility recognized

The Labour Government inherited a war damaged economy; for example it is estimated that one in three houses received some damage from enemy action, a tenth of these having been destroyed or rendered uninhabitable, over £1,000,000,000 of overseas assets had been sold, and debts nearly three times as great incurred. It also inherited the ambitious policies of the 1944 White Paper. It would have been difficult enough to achieve these ends in 'normal' circumstances, but with the battered and distorted remnants at its disposal the Government, whose responsibility in this matter everyone recognized, was faced with an almost impossible task. In the comparable situation at the end of the 1914–18 War a violent boom had ended in the longest and deepest depression yet experienced and the heroes for whom (as the slogan had it) homes were to be built, found themselves in a long dole queue. If this were not to happen again the economy had to be managed. Industry was thus subject to much more positive general as well as specific measures from 1945 onwards.

If Keynes was right, the main reason for the pre-war depression had been lack of effective demand. Consumer demand should have been increased and investment encouraged, this in itself giving rise to income creation and employment via the multiplier effect. In the post-war period the reciprocal situation obtained. Personal savings, usually 5 per cent, had risen to over 20 per cent in the war with the non-availability of goods on which to spend discretionary income and the encouragement of national saving. This accumulation of potential spending power had also taken place in businesses which had been unable to replace existing plant as it wore out. In addition Excess Profits Tax could be reclaimed after the war for the replacement of capital. There was enough demand to provide full employment and, via investment, growth, but this meant the other two objectives of the 1944 White Paper were in danger. Excess demand for a limited supply of goods and services gives rise to an increase in the general price level and a fall in the purchasing power of money. The situation is of course aggravated by demands for higher wages and this in turn leads to increased prices from the supply side.[1] Apart from the danger of this cumulative process of inflation accelerating out of control, there is the very real problem that exports become dearer, imports relatively cheaper and pressure is put on the international payments situations – exports cease to pay for imports. Conversely, and particularly important in the post-war situation of limited international reserves, the need to protect the international payments situation meant that inflation had to be kept to a minimum, even at the expense of full employment and growth. The problem was thus one of controlling the pent-up consumer demand and investment capital in order to protect the international payments situation, while at the same time trying to sustain full employment and growth.

The mechanics of control[2]

The three instruments of control available to the Government were monetary policy, fiscal policy and direct or physical controls. Monetary policy, the control of the 'liquidity' position of the economy, involving the regulation of joint stock bank lending and manipulation of interest rates, had not been used since 1932. In that year Bank Rate, the central instrument of control, was fixed at 2 per cent, to remain thus, apart from a two-month period at the beginning of the war, until 1952. A 'cheap money' policy had been retained throughout the thirties as an encouragement to recovery, and monetary policy, which had failed to control events in the inter-war period, was hardly used at all by the post-war Labour administration. After 1946 banks were required to keep their cash ratios at 8 per cent, and by convention the liquidity ratio was kept at about 30 per cent, but that was all. Such an essentially cheap money policy seems to be a contradiction if other measures were designed to deflate, but perhaps

---

[1] This is a necessarily very simple explanation of the inflationary process. For a detailed summary of 'demand pull' and 'cost push' inflation see R. G. Lipsey, *An Introduction to Positive Economics*.

[2] See *The Control of the Economy* by D. Lee in this series.

The essentially descriptive coverage of these methods of control and the relative emphasis given them by successive governments provides throughout the rest of the book the background of government economic policy in which industry existed. The reader without knowledge of the theory of monetary and fiscal policy is referred to standard texts on these subjects.

it was felt that controls, which had made monetary measures unnecessary during the war, would, in conjunction with the new-found power of fiscal policy, be sufficient in peacetime. Monetary measures were reintroduced when the Conservatives regained power in 1951, and have been used with varying degrees of emphasis in conjunction with other measures, primarily fiscal, since that time.

The acceptance of Keynesian theory and the use of policies based on it since the early forties ensured that fiscal policy, involving such things as variation in the size and structure of taxation (to act on private consumption and investment levels), and controlled flexibility in government borrowing, spending and investment policy, would be an important means of control after the war. Of the suggestions made as to how to control consumer expenditure successive governments have chosen to rely on tax policy and hire-purchase control. The 1944 White Paper argued that interference in private investment decisions was either impossible or undesirable, so that since investment had to be controlled, public investment should be carefully planned. It is important to realize here that some degree of planning by the Government is inevitable. The Government spends a great deal of money, about one-third of the national income; its borrowing, greatly increased by the enormous increase in the National Debt as the result of the two World Wars, has a marked influence on the money market; and a large proportion of total investment takes place in the public sector. But public investment is not evenly spread throughout the economy, neither is it so easy to control. It takes many forms, from large-scale investment in the nationalized industries under the direct control of the ministers concerned, to small-scale investment in, for example, water undertakings of which there are nearly 1000. The control of public investment is thus seen to be equally as difficult, a fact that was officially recognized in the White Paper on Public Investment published in 1960 (see next Chapter).

As for direct controls, their mechanisms and efficacy had already been demonstrated in wartime. The only problem was a political one; in a democracy how far are direct controls desirable in peacetime? At the time there was a great deal of controversy about the measures that should be used. It was felt on balance that fiscal measures were more likely to achieve their ends than monetary instruments and most authoritative opinion argued that an immediate abandonment of controls, as had occurred at the end of the 1914–18 War, was out of the question. Retention of controls was necessary in the period of transition from war to peace, if the experience of the years after 1918 was not to be repeated. There were, of course, marked differences of opinion as to how long such a period of transition should last and already in the General Election speeches of 1945 and increasingly in subsequent by-elections many Conservatives were campaigning for controls to be removed.

As might be expected, the Labour Government, which was to introduce legislation bringing vast areas of industry under public ownership and provide increased health and welfare services, saw controls partially as a social instrument. If controls were removed too soon, excess demand and limited supply would force up prices and, apart from the damaging inflationary effect this might have, it would mean that many goods would be beyond the income of the poorer sections of the community. It was thus a slow process of de-control which the Government used, in conjunction with fiscal measures, to enable the economy on balance to achieve a successful transition from war to peace.

Labour Government policy

The most dramatic effect on industry of government policy in the immediate post-war period was the removal of many of the basic industries into public ownership. Thus the Bank of England, coal, electricity and gas, railways and canals, road haulage, civil aviation and overseas cable and wireless were nationalized in the late 1940s, and iron and steel in the second Labour administration by 1951.

As far as the private sector was concerned the period was marked by the burden of controls, which although relaxed throughout, continued for too long in the minds of businessmen, less willing to accept government interference now that the war was over.[1] The situation was in any case not helped by the Government's policy of 'alternate tightening and slackening (of controls), following the fluctuating fortunes of the fuel situation and the balance of payments'.[2]

The controls

The list of controls, most of which had originally been imposed in the war, is indeed a formidable one.

---

[1] For an academic view condemning the continued use of controls, which it was argued brought about maldistribution of resources because of their 'inherent clumsiness', see J. Jewkes, *Ordeal by Planning*.

[2] G. D. N. Worswick, *The British Economy 1945–50*, chapter entitled 'Direct Controls'.

Private investment

Despite the views expressed in the 1944 White Paper, private investment was influenced by two controls during the period; building
licensing and control of capital issues. Building licensing was
administratively expensive but extremely effective. It was not only
used to control investment but also to relocate industry and stimulate
exports. Capital issues control, which had been reimposed for foreign
issues in 1932 and extended to all issues in 1939, was continued after
the war under the Borrowing (Control and Guarantees) Act of 1946.
Under the Act it was an offence to raise more than £50,000 in a year
by the issue of shares without the consent of the Treasury, which
acted on the advice of the Capital Issues Committee.

Although building licensing was effective, it was only partial in its
application, restricted as it was to building construction. Capital
Issues control was not very effective; application could be made in
such a way as to convince the Committee of the necessity of the project, and in any case it only dealt with one source of finance. It did not
deal with the accumulated funds of business firms themselves, neither
did it touch the institutional lenders such as the insurance companies.[1]

International trade

The pressure on the balance of payments made the control of international trade essential. The control of imports was reintroduced in
1939 under the Import, Export, and Customs Powers (Defence) Act,
and by the end of the war virtually the whole range of imported goods
was under control. Controls of imports continued throughout the
immediate post-war period, the severity of their application varying
with the state of the economy. The control of exports also took place
throughout the period. By preventing the export of machinery and
raw materials required domestically, indirect help was given to the
export drive.

Apart from these direct controls on trade the Government also
continued to control dealings in foreign exchange and the international movement of capital. Under the Exchange Control Act of
1947 all dealings in non-sterling area currencies and dealings in
sterling with non-sterling countries required the permission of the
Treasury. Also under control were capital movements to non-sterling
area countries. The most dramatic single event in this context was

---

[1] For an interesting view on the lack of control of institutional lenders
see R. Titmuss, *The Irresponsible Society*.

the devaluation of the pound in September 1949. Britain's international trading position was strengthened by reducing the price of the pound *vis-à-vis* other currencies, thus giving a stimulus to exports as their price decreased on world markets, and reducing imports which had become relatively dear.

Production

During the war, licence to manufacture a particular article had been restricted to firms already producing similar goods before 1939. In most cases control simply meant that the quantity of goods which could be manufactured in a given time period was limited. In certain cases, however, conditions as to the method of construction were laid down. For example, there were austerity restrictions limiting the amount of material to be used or prohibiting the production of luxury models. Under the 'Utility' schemes, initially concerned with the production of clothing, but extended to cover footwear, furniture, hosiery, bedding and other soft furnishings, the Government ensured the provision of reasonably priced goods of sound quality. This was partially a reaction to the tendency of manufacturers, faced with decreasing supplies of raw material and labour, to concentrate their production on higher quality goods from which a higher profit margin could be received. In some cases the specifications laid down were quite comprehensive, for example from 1943 to 1946 the entire output of furniture for civilian use consisted of utility production using specifications which not only covered minimum standards of production but also design. In any event up to 1948 manufacturers could only obtain raw materials if a certain proportion of their production came under such specifications. After that time it was left to the individual manufacturer to decide the proportion, although the fact that most utility goods were exempt from purchase tax was an indirect encouragement for him to continue to produce a reasonable share of them. Most statutory control of methods of manufacture of goods had been abolished by the end of the period.

Allocation of raw materials

An integral part of production control was the control of the allocation of raw materials. After the war the usual procedure was to retain each control until it was no longer needed. First, subsidies were removed so that prices would more accurately reflect production costs, then controls would be removed as soon as supply had increased to cope with demand at these prices. The exception to the policy

41

GOVERNMENT INTERVENTION AND INDUSTRIAL POLICY

concerned food, where prices were kept down by subsidy throughout
the period. Reduction in armament production meant that most non-
ferrous metals were freed from control almost immediately. Wool
also became more easily available at an early stage. Softwoods remained subject to allocation throughout the period, but hardwoods
were decontrolled in 1949, the same year that saw the abandonment
of cotton controls and the year before decontrol of the distribution of
steel, except for sheet steel and tinplate.

Monopoly, restrictive practice and location of industry

The 1944 White Paper recognized that if full employment was to be
maintained restrictive practices would have to be abandoned by both
sides of industry. After the war the Government therefore accepted
responsibility for controlling the detrimental aspects of monopolistic
structure. The problem of regional unemployment was faced by using
controls to influence the location of industry.[1]

Manpower

Perhaps the most important single control in the war was the control
of manpower, but in the main this was quickly abandoned after 1945.
The traditional argument of individual freedom versus State intervention had, as has been demonstrated, increasingly reflected the
acceptance of a degree of government control, but in the case of the
individual's right to work where and for whom he liked there was no
real question in people's minds. This was recognized by the Government and so there was no control of manpower in the immediate
post-war period. The only exceptions were essential work orders
which kept people in coal-mining and agriculture, and were not
removed until 1950 (the deterrent effect on new recruitment of the
existence of the controls probably meant that on balance the policy
was unsuccessful) and the temporary requirement in response to the
1947 fuel crisis that, under the Control of Engagement Order,
workers within certain age limits could leave their jobs only with the
consent of the Ministry of Labour.

Prices and wages

The successful operation of the various production controls obviously
required control of prices. Prices of consumer goods were controlled
under two Acts of Parliament, the Prices of Goods Act of 1939 and
the Goods and Services (Price Control) Act of 1941. In 1948, the

---

[1] For detailed coverage of these topics see *Monopoly* and *Regional
Planning and the Location of Industry*, both books in this series.

year in which there was a marked relaxation of production controls following the appointment of an Examiner of Controls by the President of the Board of Trade,[1] an attempt was made to tighten control of prices. A degree of success was achieved in slowing the rate of increase of retail prices in the year following the various Price Control Orders of March 1948. A parallel policy of restraining wages[2] met with union co-operation and a wage-freeze occurred in the same period. A return to previous trends in prices and wages followed, accentuated by the devaluation of sterling in September 1949, but no subsequent machinery was developed to control them further.

Conclusion

Thus, under a system involving the sort of controls that would previously have been unacceptable to industry in peacetime, the economy made its initial transition from war to peace more successfully than could have been expected. Average industrial production increased by 40 per cent, the volume of exports was up by nearly 80 per cent, compared with a 30 per cent increase in the volume of imports, and, perhaps most remarkable of all, the level of employment, save for a few weeks during the fuel crisis of 1947, was higher than the most optimistic wartime forecasters had thought possible in peace time.[3] By the end of the period the Labour Government had completed a substantial programme of nationalization and welfare provision, and many of the controls which the individual had suffered for the sake of the efficient execution of the war and stability in the post-war period, had been removed. There were reasons for this, not the least being that neither Germany nor Japan had yet entered world markets. There had been temporary crises, but growth had been achieved and at the end of the period there was even a breathing space provided by a surplus on the balance of payments. Industry could look forward to the fifties with a certain amount of optimism, for controls were being relaxed, and the less obtrusive general economic policies were in the main providing the stability essential to business expectations. Certainly Winston Churchill's 1948 prophecy of a nation moving towards 'bankruptcy and privation' had not been borne out.

---

[1] A large proportion of controls were relaxed or abandoned that year in Harold Wilson's 'bonfire of controls'.

[2] Both these measures reflected the White Paper on Personal Incomes, Costs and Prices issued February 1948.

[3] Throughout the figure remained at less than 400,000. Beveridge had thought 550,000 the minimum practicable.

7.
1950–1961 RETURN TO THE MARKET-PLACE

Initial survey

Despite the trend towards decontrol outlined in the previous chapter, the last year of Labour administration was still characterized by physical controls. The 'massive permanent legacy of official direction over economic processes'[1] left behind by the war, was still very much in evidence. Frustration was thus partially responsible for the return of a Conservative Government committed to a liberalization of the economy. By the autumn of 1951 the 'popular mood was one which favoured the objective of more consumer choice even at the expense of a little social injustice'.[2]

In fact pressure on the balance of payments meant that the Conservatives tightened controls on coming to office, but the period as a whole saw the dismantling of the great majority of controls so that the management of the economy relied mainly on fiscal, and increasingly, monetary measures. This return to the market-place was only partially successful in achieving the now accepted post-war economic objectives. Activity fluctuated, with high points in 1954 and 1958, and this meant that the unemployment rate was not maintained at its exceptionally low level. The period was essentially one of full employment, however, since the fluctuations in activity never resembled pre-war intensity, and even in the less active periods the overall unemployment rate was only in the order of 2 per cent. Prices on the whole increased at about the same rate as under the Labour administration, although the rate of increase reflected the fluctuations in activity, and some components, notably food and rents,[3] increased at a faster rate, while the reverse was true of, for example, clothing and household durables. Finally, despite the successive removal of barriers to convertibility which made the pound more freely exchangeable in foreign exchange markets and therefore

---

[1] G. C. Allen, *The Structure of Industry in Britain.*
[2] Andrew Shonfield, *British Economic Policy Since the War.*
[3] Especially after decontrol under the 1957 Rent Act.

more susceptible to speculation in time of external pressure, a surplus was more often than not achieved on the current account of the balance of payments throughout the fifties.

The least successful aspect of government policy during the period was undoubtedly the failure to stimulate enough growth in the economy; and it was this relatively slow rate of increase in national wealth compared with other European countries that finally brought the Conservatives back from the freedom of the market, and to the recognition that more planning was necessary than they had previously thought.

Freedom from control

The Korean War, which forced up world prices and stimulated a concentration on rearmament at home, was mainly responsible for the 1951 deficit on the balance of payments current account which faced the Conservatives when they came to power. Their reaction was to tighten controls, imports were successively reduced, new hire-purchase restrictions were imposed, banks were ordered to restrict credit, the Capital Issues Committee was to be less permissive, the travel allowance was reduced to £25 and, under the Notification of Vacancies Order, it became illegal for employers to acquire labour other than through the Labour Exchanges, to which all vacancies had to be notified. But as soon as the storm had been weathered the Government set about the task of decontrol with unconcealed enthusiasm.

Food de-rationing, starting with eggs in the spring of 1953, was completed with the freeing of meat by the middle of the next year. The Government stopped buying imports and re-opened the commodity markets; by the end of the period State importing had almost disappeared, along with import controls. Building licences were abolished by the end of 1954. Although the limit on new issues under capital issues control was limited to £10,000 from 1956 to 1958, control was in fact suspended in February 1959. The control of industrial location and monopolistic and restrictive practices however increased during the period.[1]

The movement towards the free convertibility of the pound on foreign exchange markets, conforming to international agreements governing monetary and commercial arrangements between countries

---

[1] See *Monopoly* and *Regional Planning and the Location of Industry* in this series.

which dated back to the war years, was perhaps the most far-reaching example of the Government's liberalization policy. With the movement of the Bank of England into unofficial markets, using the country's resources to support the pound, the penultimate step to convertibility had been taken as early as 1955. By 1958 sterling was officially convertible except for residents of the sterling area. The danger of such a policy is, of course, that the domestic economy is more susceptible to outside pressure. Thus the slow rate of growth in the economy in this period can be partially attributed to caution on the part of the Government, having committed itself to less direct control in the international exchange markets and not wanting to encourage expansion which might prove inflationary. Speculation against the pound (the selling of sterling for other currencies when it is felt that devaluation might take place and a profit could be made from buying sterling again after it has happened, a process which itself puts downward pressure on the price of the pound) was the primary cause of the balance of payments crisis of 1955 and again played an important part when sterling was under pressure during the Suez crisis in 1956 and from strong rumours of devaluation in 1957. It is not surprising therefore that the surplus of over £300,000,000 in 1958 was considered more as a windfall for the reserves than as a safety margin for the encouragement of investment at home.

Denationalization
The continued existence of the mixed economy was assured when the Conservative Government retained the majority of the nationalized industries under State ownership. There was some concession to private enterprise however. Most of the steel industry was returned to private ownership, along with a part of the road haulage industry; structural changes, essentially de-centralizing, took place in electricity and on the railways; and more competition was allowed in the field of civil aviation. The need for competition for the sake of efficiency is questionable, where, for example, oligopolistic structure simply leads to duplication of resources and competitive waste. It is difficult, however, to think of an alternative stimulus to the efficiency which many people think is lacking in State enterprise.

The revival of monetary control
As has been indicated, a return to the freedom of the market within a managed economy involves the use of monetary measures. Thus Bank Rate was reintroduced as an instrument of control, fluctuating

with activity rates and reaching its highest level of 7 per cent in the crisis of Autumn 1957. A further control on credit was the 'directive' given by the Bank of England that the traditional 30 per cent liquidity ratio should be adhered to. In April 1960 a system of 'special deposits' was introduced. This in effect meant a freezing of a proportion of the banks' liquid assets so that credit had to be restricted. Additional reliance was placed on the power of interest rates, when local authorities were forced on to the market for their capital funds in 1955. The Public Works Loan Board which had provided finance up to that time (from 1953 the local authorities were allowed to go to the market) provided money now only if the local authority could not raise it on the market; and in any case the market rate was paid for such loans. There was also dissatisfaction felt by the Government at the way the Exchequer had since 1956 been supplying the nationalized industries with the capital they had been finding difficult to raise.

By the end of the period it was recognized that too much reliance had been placed on monetary instruments. The Bank Rate did have a psychological effect both at home and particularly abroad in that it was acceptable as an indication of government policy at any given time. By itself, however, interest-rate policy was not seen to be very effective. This view was put forward in the Radcliffe Report[1] which argued that domestically 'the main effect of the restriction of bank credit was to drive frustrated borrowers to other sources' and that internationally 'Bank Rate . . . *if reinforced by other means* . . . can serve to restore confidence in sterling, and reassure financial opinion abroad that the authorities will not remain quiescent in the face of inflationary dangers' [my italics].

Fiscal policy

The realization by the end of the period that the use of public investment was both impracticable and undesirable as an instrument of control has already been mentioned (see page 38). The 1960 White Paper argued that, for example, stable expansion and the provision of social services should not be subject to short-term variation of investment plans. This was not, however, before such a policy had already been used; for example a number of cuts in the investment programme of nationalized undertakings accompanied the increase in Bank Rate to 7 per cent in the autumn of 1957.

As for private investment this was left increasingly to interest rate

---

[1] 'Report on the Working of the Monetary System', 1959.

and taxation policy, as direct controls, save for those concerned with the location of industry, were removed. Private investment was encouraged in general or discriminatively by various forms of tax relief. There were three main types. The first was the depreciation allowance which permitted the businessman to deduct from each year's taxable income a proportion of the cost of capital outlay. The length of life of the capital equipment and the proportion of the total cost allowed were agreed between individual businessmen and the Inland Revenue. The second, originally introduced by Stafford Cripps in 1949, although removed by Hugh Gaitskill two years later, was the initial allowance, which increased the depreciation allowance in the first year. This allowance varied with type of investment. The third, originally introduced by Butler in 1954, was the new investment allowance, which allowed the businessman to set a given percentage of the cost of capital equipment against taxable income in the first year in addition to the depreciation allowance.

In controlling consumer demand emphasis continued to be given to tax rates and hire-purchase regulations. There are two ways of controlling hire purchase; by restricting the availability of funds used for this purpose and by regulating the terms of agreement. The Radcliffe Committee found that the first of these was not being effectively pursued. The regulation of terms by the Board of Trade does however have immediate and impressive effect. The unfortunate aspect of the use of such a policy is the directional nature of its incidence; the motor and consumer durable industries particularly suffer in this respect.

The fact that fiscal changes take place only once a year, on Budget Day, is an obvious limitation to their effectiveness. Not only are sections of the economy distorted just before the Budget as individuals and business firms try to cushion themselves against expected changes, but since conditions are changing continuously, measures can become outdated long before the next Budget is due. It is possible for Chancellors to introduce Special Budgets, but such procedure is unusual, is associated with emergencies and is thus avoided when marginal adjustment only is required. Its very use might provoke undesired opinion as to the state of the economy. The first sign of official recognition of this limitation came with the 1961 Budget in which it was proposed that a surcharge of up to 10 per cent of existing tax rates could be imposed on all indirect taxes at any time of the year. This measure is known as the 'regulator' and has been used by various Chancellors since that time. It is argued by many economists, however, that more could be done to make fiscal measures continuously relevant to the economic situation.

Savings

One way to affect consumption is, of course, to stimulate changes in saving habits. An obvious instrument is National Savings. Net saving decreased after the war and in the early fifties was sometimes negative. There was a marked increase at the end of the period which coincided with the introduction of Premium bonds by Harold Macmillan, although statistics show that most of the increase was due to other forms of saving (particularly National Savings Certificates and Defence Bonds). However there is no doubt that the Premium Bond was a successful addition to the National Savings range and many people feel that more could be done to absorb surplus purchasing power with a more imaginative National Savings programme.

Conclusion

Despite talk by Butler of doubling the standard of living in twenty-five years,[1] and cries of 'We've never had it so good!' from Harold Macmillan (and for the majority of the population he was right), a comparison with other European countries showed quite convincingly that Britain's rate of economic growth since the war had been too slow. The transition had been made from war to peace, full employment had been maintained, but the pressure on the balance of payments had meant that investment had not taken place at a comparable rate with other industrial nations. By the end of the period the Conservative Government was beginning to realize that more control than had been practised in their early years of office would be necessary if the country was to increase its national wealth at the rate thought desirable, but which had not as yet been attained. There had been an attempt to control wages and prices in the later fifties and talk was increasingly of the need, in a full employment economy, to raise labour productivity and tie wages to such productivity increases. Perhaps, too, a more realistic assessment of the country's world position, especially after the Suez episode at the end of 1956, was leading to a counting of the 'true economic cost of international commitments which carried a traditional stamp'.[2] In simple terms, the

---

[1] This of course sounded a lot better than the 2·8 per cent average annual growth rate on which it is based.

[2] Andrew Shonfield, *British Economic Policy since the War*.

maintenance of troops overseas put added strain on the balance of payments by virtue of the foreign exchange required to pay for them. In any event the sixties were to see an increase in central direction as initially the Conservatives, and subsequently the Labour Government committed themselves to plan for growth and expansion.

8.
1962–1970 PLANNING FOR GROWTH

Initial survey

The pressure on the Balance of Payments requiring periodic deflation-ary measures had led to what became known as the 'stop–go' policy of the Conservative Government in the late fifties. Investment had been curtailed and growth had been painfully slow. From 1955 to 1962 Gross Investment as a percentage of Gross National Product was 17 per cent in this country as against, for example, 28 per cent in West Germany, 23 per cent in Italy and 20 per cent in France.[1] The annual average rate of increase of Gross National Product for the years 1955 to 1960 was 2·8 per cent in this country compared with 6·3 per cent in Western Germany, 5·5 per cent in Italy and 4·6 per cent in France. The figure for Japan was 9·7 per cent.[2] Thus it was that first the Conservatives and then the Labour Government introduced a greater degree of general control, involving closer links with both sides of industry, the introduction of new institutions, and various rationalizations of the machinery of government, in an attempt to foster growth. In the event the sixties proved as depressing as ever. Throughout the period and for many reasons including an initially over-valued pound, speculation both at home and abroad, industrial disputes, particularly those directly affecting trade such as the 1966 Seamen's Strike, the Middle East Crisis causing the closing of the Suez Canal and the use of economic sanctions against Rhodesia,[3] the almost continuous strain on the balance of payments was such as to bring about a succession of deflationary 'packages' such as the 'July measures' of 1966. Devaluation of the pound in November 1967 did not bring the degree of relief required, and the borrowing of vast sums from the International Monetary Fund

---

[1] For further comparison see the Brookings Institution Study, *Britain's Economic Prospects*.

[2] *Economic Growth 1960–1970*, O.E.C.D.

[3] It is important to realize that these often marginal pressures would not in themselves have been so important if the country's underlying economic position had been one of strength.

51

only served to reinforce the need to attain a surplus in our international trading account almost at the cost of all else. Mr Roy Jenkins's first Budget in 1968 took over £900 million out of consumers' pockets in extra taxation. A year later the emphasis was still on deflation as the Government continued to have 'little room for manœuvre in planning its economic strategy'.[1]

Through the years various scapegoats have been blamed for Britain's troubles. These have included the maintenance of an overvalued pound, excessive government spending on social capital and benefits, and on defence, too much assistance to underdeveloped countries, unenterprising management, particularly in its failure to introduce new techniques and sustain its share of the world export markets (it is only fair to say, however, that although this share is falling, a greater proportion of this country's, as compared with any other's national product is exported and that perhaps the Government could do more to stimulate exports while paying lip service to international agreements such as G.A.T.T.), overfull employment and the currently fashionable irresponsibility of the workers.[2] But whatever the reasons, the fact remains that successive governments have found it almost impossible to achieve all the objectives set out in the 1944 White Paper. Perhaps this is not surprising; the objectives themselves conflict with one another so that some compromise was necessary in any case. External pressures and the use of sterling by other countries for their reserves have meant that domestic policy has always been subject to severe restraint, and the instruments of government control still have to be refined. Controversy continues as to the correct emphasis to give to the various measures governments can use. To many people the history of the sixties has simply illustrated that the movement away from the market-place was wrong.[3] Those people on the other hand who felt that the formal relationships between the Government, industry and unions developed within the framework of the new machinery of central direction should remain and be extended were dealt a severe

---

[1] Richard Bailey, *Managing the British Economy*.

[2] Roy Jenkins' use of the 1969 Budget Speech as a policy statement on industrial relations involving the need quickly to implement proposals in the White Paper, 'In Place of Strife' gave undue emphasis to this particular cause of economic difficulty and inevitably led to an immediate worsening of the relationship between the Government and the unions.

[3] See J. Jewkes, *A New Ordeal by Planning*.

blow by the return in 1970 of a Conservative Government committed to less interference in the industrial field.

The changing structure of control

Before a more detailed summary is given of the development of government control in the sixties, it is valuable to examine the structure of control, both as it existed at the beginning of the period and as it developed, with the introduction of new institutions and changes in the function of established ones.

The pragmatic development of government intervention meant that a large number of different bodies was responsible for the various aspects of government economic policy. These ranged from the central departments, through the local authorities, to various independent corporations, commissions and boards. The most important were the central departments, and their functions and responsibilities as they were at the beginning of the period are dealt with first. In many cases these functions have continued to the present day and can be considered to have done so unless a change is mentioned later in the chapter.[1]

The Trade and Industry Departments

Particular departments sponsor their own industries. This involves dealing with all aspects of the relationships between the Government and the industry or section of the industry. For example, the Ministry of Agriculture, Fisheries and Food protects land for agricultural use against the demands of other bodies, promotes improvements in farming methods, directly encourages the production of more food (via price supports), rationalizes marketing and, since it absorbed the Ministry of Food in 1955, regulates the standard of food reaching the consumer. This involves being responsible for such bodies as the Milk Marketing Board and the White Fish Authority. An important part of the work of sponsoring is to ensure that the claims of the industry are well represented at Cabinet level, especially claims to the limited finance provided by the Treasury.

In 1960 there were five of these specific departments; the Ministry of Agriculture, Fisheries and Food, the Department of Agriculture for Scotland, the Ministry of Transport, the Ministry of Power and the Ministry of Aviation. Three other Departments, the

---

[1] The same principle has been adopted in revising the book; the most recent changes in structure and function being dealt with in Chapter 9.

Ministry of Works, the Ministry of Health and the General Post Office took responsibility for their own sectors, but were not officially trade and industry departments. All these, along with the Board of Trade, part of whose function is to sponsor those industries not covered elsewhere, were known as the 'Production Departments'. These, together with the Ministry of Labour, which had responsibility for manpower throughout industry, and the Treasury, which was responsible for co-ordination and economic policy and which was the most powerful in that it held the purse-strings, formed the main framework of economic control. But other departments also had some economic functions. Among these were the Department of Scientific and Industrial Research, the Office of the Registrar of Restrictive Trading Agreements, the Overseas Departments concerned with trading agreements, and the Home Office miscellaneously responsible for, among other things, the control of immigrants and naturalization of aliens, the granting of licences for scientific experiments on animals and the administration of the State-controlled brewery and public houses in Carlisle.[1]

The Board of Trade

The Board of Trade which is the oldest of the trade and industry departments, also fulfilled other functions. It was responsible, with the Treasury, for general trade policy and, with the overseas departments, for negotiating trade agreements. It was the department mostly concerned with the promotion of exports, providing information and particularly important, export insurance in its Export Credits Guarantee Department. Through the years it acquired various regulatory functions concerning commercial practice. This involved administration of legislation concerned with, for example, patents, weights and measures, bankruptcy, and more recently monopoly and restrictive practices. The Board of Trade was also responsible, together with the Treasury, the Ministry of Housing and Local Government and the Ministry of Labour, for the Government's location of industry policy. Finally, as the department responsible for industry generally, it was in charge of such things as administration of tariffs and import–export controls, promotion of various aspects of industry including productivity, reorganization, standardization and design, and the provision of statistical information about trade and industry including the censuses of production and distribution.

---

[1] These are now to be transferred to private ownership. See page 82.

The Treasury

This is the central department of the civil service and is responsible for the regulation and collection of taxation, the control of public expenditure, monetary policy and exchange control. At the beginning of the sixties it was also traditionally the department responsible for overall economic direction. In effect, before the 1939–45 War this simply meant that the Treasury had the last word at Cabinet level when conflict arose between the economic policies of other departments. Little was done, as has been seen, to instigate positive policy and in the economic co-ordination carried out by the Treasury a great deal of weight was given to 'financial considerations'.

This overemphasis on finance was partially the reason for the Government removing economic direction from the Treasury in 1941, when it established the Lord President's Committee. The staff of this committee were taken from the economic section of the Central Economic Information Service. This was a group of professional economists and statisticians drawn mainly from the Universities, who had been assembled at the beginning of the war to serve the newly created Economic Policy Committee of the Cabinet. There remained the statistical section which became the Central Statistical Office providing authoritative and consistent statistics for the policy-makers. It is important to remember that official statistics were not very well developed up to this time. For example, the first official estimates of National Income were only made in 1940 (this was mainly due to the efforts of Keynes and other 'temporaries'). The work of the C.S.O. has expanded and by the sixties it was providing original statistics and estimates drawing on a wide range of sources including such private institutions as the National Institute for Economic and Social Research.

In the immediate post-war period the responsibility for planning remained with the Lord President, but was transferred to the newly created Minister of Economic Affairs (Sir Stafford Cripps) in the atmosphere of crisis in 1947. When Sir Stafford Cripps moved to the Treasury with the resignation of Dr. Dalton as Chancellor it appeared that responsibility for planning was again with the Treasury. The process was completed in 1953 with the transfer of the Economic Section to the Treasury when its Director became Chief Economic Adviser to the Government. By then, of course, anti-planning was at its height and at the end of the decade, apart from a brief period when Harold Macmillan and Sir Edward Boyle were at the Treasury, the function of the Economic Section of the Treasury had become that of mere co-ordinator.

Much criticism has been levelled at the Treasury concerning the way it put financial and monetary considerations before all else, and was therefore seen to be responsible for the successive bouts of deflationary measures as it sought to stabilize prices and protect sterling. There was also concern as to the limited number of specialist economists and statisticians working in the Treasury and other government departments.[1] Criticisms of the structure of the Treasury were expressed in the Plowden Report[2] and this led to a reorganization on a more functional basis. The defects in the system which were found by the Plowden Committee coincided with the views of those who argued for greater control of the economy at that time, and for new institutions to aid such control. There were two main deficiencies the Report argued: decisions on government expenditure were still taken on an *ad hoc* basis without reference to public need or resource availability, and there was no real machinery co-ordinating the demands of the various sectors in any positive way. In the event the planners had their way, but introduction of new machinery and the will to make it work have not so far proved strong enough to cope with the country's economic difficulties. Indeed, as has been said, many people have reacted against the increased control which has seemingly brought little success.

The National Economic Development Council

The first institutional manifestation of Conservative Government change of heart came with the establishment of the N.E.D.C. which first met in March 1962. A greater growth-rate was to be achieved with the help of this organization which would specifically involve both sides of industry and take responsibility for the provision of long-term plans and forecasts. Organized industry in the form of the three main employers associations (these later merged becoming the Confederation of British Industry, in order to present a united front at meetings, see page 22) and after some reticence the T.U.C., agreed to participate in what was termed 'indicative planning'. The original

---

[1] In 1960 there were less than 100 economists and statisticians employed by the Government. The Treasury, the main employer of economists, had about a dozen at that time. See J. W. Grove, *Government and Industry in Britain*.

[2] The White Paper, 'Control of Government Expenditure', 1961.

Council had six management members, six unionists, two representatives of the nationalized industries, two independent members and the three Ministers most concerned, the Chancellor of the Exchequer, the Minister of Labour and the President of the Board of Trade. The Director General was named as Sir Robert Shone, a distinguished economist and up to that time executive member of the Iron and Steel Board.

The N.E.D.C. office was divided into two sections. The Economic Division was to be responsible for providing estimates on which a growth programme could be based and was concerned therefore with such things as isolating obstacles to faster growth, suggesting ways of removing inefficiency and making better use of the country's resources. The Industrial Division was to achieve a closer liaison between the Government and industry.

In February 1963 the N.E.D.C. published a growth programme.[1] This was perhaps done somewhat hastily, especially when it is remembered that the Office had started from nothing just a year before. It studied the implications of a 4 per cent rate of growth on the various sectors of the economy. This rate of growth was chosen as being realistic enough to succeed in the light of the 3 per cent growth rate at the time and also coincided with estimates of European growth potential. Although it was adopted as a target by industry and politicians alike, as might be expected, the Treasury remained quietly sceptical. The Report itself was in two parts; an industrial inquiry which assessed the effect of such a growth rate on a selection of industries, followed by the implications for the economy as a whole. The information had been obtained quickly and was based on the acceptance of given assumptions such as similar growth rates elsewhere and the probability of soon entering the Common Market, although de Gaulle had vetoed Britain's entry but a month before the Report was published. On balance, however, it was a worth-while exercise. For the first time official estimates were based on data inherent in which was an assumption of a given overall growth rate, and what emerged about potential bottlenecks enabled the N.E.D.C. to issue a policy report in April 1963.[2]

This Report was divided into a number of sections each dealing with a particular aspect of the economy and recommending measures necessary to obtain faster growth. Among the topics covered were

---

[1] *Growth of the U.K. Economy 1961–66.*
[2] *Conditions Favourable to Faster Growth.*

Education and Growth, Taxation, and Prices and Incomes. But although policy-making was marginally affected by the Report, in particular with respect to regional policy, the Government took little real notice of its arguments. There was certainly no co-ordination of policy at Cabinet level in an attempt to work within the framework of the N.E.D.C. recommendations, and by the time of the 1964 Election attention was focused more on the new machinery promised by the Labour Party. One of the main reasons for the relative lack of success of the N.E.D.C., apart from the continued suspicion of 'planning' by many people in government and industry, was undoubtedly its independence. It was not a government department, and it did not have free access to the statistics of government departments. Thus it carried too little political weight to ensure a fair hearing for itself.[1]

The Economic Development Committees
Beginning in 1964 the Industrial Division set up a series of Economic Development Committees for particular industries with the intention of formalizing the links between the N.E.D.C. and industry. Each committee consists of representatives of management, the unions and the appropriate government department, together with a few independent members. There were nine E.D.C.s established before the 1964 General Election including those for Electronics, Mechanical Engineering, Chemicals and Distribution.

The Department of Economic Affairs
Two days after the 1964 General Election the Labour Government established the Department of Economic Affairs under the First Secretary of State and Secretary of State for Economic Affairs, George Brown. It had no executive functions, but was responsible for overall medium and long-term planning involving the efficient use of physical resources. Short-term and financial policy remained the prerogative of the Treasury. The Department was originally organized into four interrelated groups.

The Economic Planning Group was responsible for the formulation of what became known as the National Plan. The vital difference

---

[1] For an explanation of the continued existence of the N.E.D.C. through all the subsequent changes in the machinery of planning see 'Why Neddy Survived', Sir Frederick Catherwood, *Lloyds Bank Review*, April 1971.

between the approach to planning of the two governments is brought out in this quote from the first D.E.A. Report published in January 1965: 'This group is working on the foundations laid by the N.E.D.C. Its plans will, however, be full statements of government policy to which Ministers will be committed in framing their own departmental programmes.' The N.E.D.C. provided the greater part of the staff for this group from its Economic Section, but with the Minister of Economic Affairs at its head instead of the Chancellor, and including the newly appointed Minister of Technology[1] and the Industrial Adviser to the Government, it continued as part of the planning machine.

The Industrial Policy Group of the D.E.A. was to consider the obstacles to growth in individual industries and would work in close collaboration with the E.D.C.s which were to be retained and extended.

The Economic Co-ordination Group was responsible for prices and incomes, public expenditure and external economic policy as well as the implementation of the growth plan.

Finally the Regional Policy Group was responsible for economic and physical aspects of regional planning, including effects on industry, employment and land use. This meant that the Board of Trade was relieved of some of the responsibility for overall policy, but it still administered incentives for companies setting up in Development Areas.

The Department underwent various changes in its lifetime, perhaps the most important being the loss of responsibility for productivity, prices and incomes. In 1965 the National Board for Prices and Incomes was created under the chairmanship of Aubrey Jones. Responsibility for co-ordination of a productivity, prices and incomes policy remained with the Department until April 1968 when it was taken over by the extended and renamed Labour Ministry, the Department of Employment and Productivity. In its final form the D.E.A. was organized into three main groups. The Industrial Group, which consulted with industry through the N.E.D.C. and the E.D.C.s, was responsible for the Industrial Reorganization Corporation set up in 1966 to promote selected mergers where such a change in structure would lead to the greater efficiency necessary to withstand international competition. The Corporation was responsible for various structural changes, the two largest examples of regrouping

---

[1] This was Frank Cousins who had previously sat in the Council as a T.U.C. representative.

being the G.E.C./A.E.I. merger, where the Corporation supported an opposed takeover, and the agreed merger between B.M.C. and Leyland where the Corporation provided a loan of £25 million for immediate rationalization and development. However, it disappointed many people, who saw it as the 'financial nucleus for major public initiatives in industry',[1] and indeed its policy was questionable if it was simply a case of 'find the most efficient firm in Britain and merge the rest of them into it'.[2]

The Economic Group was concerned with advanced research into the problem of resource allocation, particularly the problem of switching resources to assist the balance of payments situation in the medium and long term. The Regional Group was responsible for co-ordinating regional policy.[3]

The Ministry of Technology

The optimism and enthusiasm which gave rise to the D.E.A. was also responsible for the creation of the new Ministry of Technology which was to revolutionize the economy by encouraging the use of advanced technological processes in British industry. It immediately became the sponsoring department for four industries; computers, machine tools, electronics and telecommunications, and subsequently extended its sponsorship to cover almost all electrical and engineering industries, including motors, aircraft and shipbuilding. It took from the Board of Trade and other departments responsibility for research and development in engineering, atomic energy, aircraft, missiles and radar.

In July 1966 the Ministry set up the National Computing Centre in order to standardize programming and advise on the training of programmers and systems analysts. The Ministry also short-circuits the procedure for adopting up-to-date methods by buying the latest machines and lending them for free assessment by potential users who would not perhaps have been prepared to buy a machine untried. The Ministry is also concerned with increasing the efficiency of management by the introduction of modern methods and techniques.

In January 1967 the Central Advisory Council for Science and Technology was set up to advise the Government on the most

---

[1] *Britain's Economic Prospects*, the Brooking's Institution Study, p. 388 n.

[2] *Op. cit.*, p. 321.

[3] For details of this aspect of the Department's work see *Regional Planning and Location of Industry*.

effective use and development of the country's scientific and technical resources. Although this country spends more on scientific and industrial research and development (R and D), than any other except America and Russia, it is renownedly lacking when it comes to commercial exploitation. Among the Council's recommendations in its first Report[1] were that R and D and marketing should be more closely associated, and in particular that new research projects should be based on analysis of the market; that there should be an increased flow of qualified manpower into all levels of industrial management with more scientists in production and marketing, and that a closer relationship should exist between government agencies and industry.

The Department of Employment and Productivity

In April 1968 the Ministry of Labour took over responsibility for Prices and Incomes and became the Department of Employment and Productivity. Its previous functions, such as the provision of Labour Exchanges and the Youth Employment Service and the operation of government vocational training schemes were retained, while its new title and responsibility for prices and incomes emphasized the importance of labour productivity in the pursuit of growth without inflation.

Centralization and extension of the provision of statistics

In 1968, in response to the need for more reliable statistics as a basis for planning decisions, the Government took steps to improve the 'timeliness, range and compatibility' of official statistics. Although statistics had been improving, particularly since the last war, they had developed on a departmental basis, with any co-ordination the function of the C.S.O. as it prepared publications such as the 'Monthly Digest of Statistics', using the departments as sources. The C.S.O. was now to have a new key role in the Government statistical system. Four new units were to be set up in the C.S.O. concerned respectively with the best use of computers, rationalization of classification and definition between departments, co-ordination of the collection of raw materials to avoid duplication, and planning and integrating the whole of the Government's future statistical programme.

On the 1st January 1969 the new Business Statistics Office was established out of the Board of Trade Census Office. It is staffed by the Board of Trade but policy is decided by an inter-departmental

---

[1] *Technological Innovation in Britain.*

management committee under the chairmanship of the Director of the C.S.O. It is to establish a Central Register of Businesses, a mammoth task, already begun by the Board of Trade and the Department of Employment and Productivity when it was the Ministry of Labour, involving details of some two million establishments. Each firm will be coded by location, industrial classification and size. When this has been achieved the Register will not only act as a source of information for government inquiries and a basis for sample surveys, but the cumulative collection of information which will be stored in the computer will enable a new system of industrial statistics to be introduced. The traditional quinquennial Census of Production which has served as the basis for economic indicators like the Index of Industrial Production since 1907, will gradually be replaced by the collection of figures at quarterly or even monthly intervals. The first of the new quarterly inquiries dealt with printing and publishing. The increased though rationalized form-filling might prove irksome to management initially, but the resulting provision of comparable up-to-date figures enabling each firm better to plan ahead, should more than compensate for this.

The 1960s saw several shifts in the responsibility for economic control between various government departments. The movement away from the Treasury tentatively begun by the Conservatives, was most marked immediately after the creation of the Department of Economic Affairs which stood for growth and dynamism under the control of the effervescent George Brown. As it became increasingly apparent that it was necessary to subordinate growth to the ever-present requirement of balancing the international accounts, emphasis necessarily shifted back to the Treasury and, after April 1968, the Department of Employment and Productivity. It is significant that the title of First Secretary of State, previously associated with the Secretary of State for Economic Affairs at the D.E.A., was subsequently held by the Minister at the Department of Employment and Productivity, Barbara Castle.

The creation of new organizations and changes in the function of existing departments did not make it easy for businessmen to know what was happening, especially when there was real or apparent overlap of responsibility by the various planning agencies, only some of which might reasonably have been expected to continue to function. In the event further changes were to take place under the Labour administration in the autumn of 1969 and a year later under the new Conservative Government.

Further changes in the machinery of government

In October 1969 the Ministry of Technology, under Mr Anthony Wedgewood Benn, was expanded to incorporate the Ministry of Power and take over much of the industrial responsibilities of the Board of Trade. The Ministry of Housing and Local Government together with the Ministry of Transport were now the responsibility of the Secretary of State for Local Government and Regional Planning, Mr Anthony Crosland, who was also responsible for regional development. As had been forecast, the Department of Economic Affairs ceased to exist. Medium and long term economic assessment and coordination reverted to the Treasury which was now responsible for the work of the retained National Economic Development Office.

The enlarged Ministry of Technology, having acquired further sponsorship functions from the old Board of Trade, was now responsible for virtually the whole of private industry, and, via its incorporation of the Ministry of Power, the nationalized industries as well. It was responsible for the industrial aspects of planning. It also took over responsibilities for regional economic development including regional employment policies and the location of industry previously held by the D.E.A., together with the Board of Trade's residual regional responsibilities concerning such things as incentives to firms moving to Development Areas (see page 59). Finally, with the immediate break up of the D.E.A. the Industrial Development Corporation became the responsibility of what was termed this 'virtual "Ministry for Industry"'.[1]

The Secretary of State for Local Government and Regional Planning was now responsible for the separate but subordinate Ministries of Housing and Local Government and Transport, together with the regional economic planning councils and boards previously with the D.E.A. The further diminished Board of Trade was now primarily responsible for overseas trade and export promotion, including those industries such as civil aviation, shipping, hotels and insurance, associated with invisible earnings. At home it was to concentrate on commerce rather than industry, retaining responsibility for the regulation of commercial practices. However, it was to continue to sponsor the distributive and retail trades, printing and publishing, and the film industry.

These changes, which gave the new super Ministry of Technology

[1] *The Times* October 6th 1969.

an almost comprehensive coverage of industry, were greeted cautiously by businessmen. While welcoming them if it meant that they would increase the government's awareness of the problems of industry, they feared greater interference by the government. For example, the use of the I.R.C. to force rationalization to suit the needs of industry as a whole, including the nationalized industries, was more likely now that one Ministry was responsible for overall industrial policy. Because of this emphasis on concentration of responsibility for industry they were nevertheless changes which could have made the relationship between government and the industry more profitable.

Changes in public ownership

With the acceptance of the mixed economy by both parties a change of government only brings marginal changes in public ownership; it is of course unfortunate that the iron and steel industry finds itself on the margin. The Iron and Steel Board which had exercised a general supervision over the industry since its return to the private sector in 1953, had not been noted for its energy and enthusiasm for the task, and so it was not surprising that the fourteen major companies, producing 90 per cent of Britain's crude steel and employing 70 per cent of the labour force, were brought back into public ownership by the Labour Government in 1967.

Under the Transport Act of 1962 the various remaining state-owned services were grouped together under the Transport Holding Company. In November 1965, a service from London to Glasgow saw the beginning of the joint use of road and rail services for the transport of goods. Plans for freight-liners had first been announced in the 1963 report *Reshaping British Railways*, and eventually the Government intends to establish a national freight organization connecting all the main industrial and commercial centres of Britain with Ireland and the Continent. The 1968 Transport Act established a new publicly owned authority, the National Freight Corporation, which has the duty of providing a first-class integrated system of door-to-door transport, based mainly on the use of freight liners. As with the Railways Board, the Corporation has the financial duty of paying its way, although grants will be paid in both cases to cover unavoidable losses. In the case of the railways this means the provision of socially desirable but unprofitable passenger services, and for the National Freight Corporation responsibility for 'sundries' traffic which was previously one of the heaviest loss-making services provided by the railways in wasteful competition with British Road

Services Parcels Ltd. Other aspects of this rationalizing Act dealt with changes in licensing control, reorganization of passenger transport and development of inland waterways for leisure purposes. Separate legislation passed control of London Transport to the Greater London Council. The Government also intended to reorganize the ports.

In October 1968 the Post Office opened the Giro banking service. This system, which already existed in Japan and most states of Western Europe, with which latter countries an international transfer system is now available, provides a cheap method of paying bills based on the computerized holding of all accounts in a single centre. As with a normal bank account wages can be paid directly into the Giro system with obvious advantages to the firm in terms of efficiency and security. The Giro did not initially provide overdraft or loan facilities although a scheme was introduced later.

Monetary policy

The full range of monetary instruments was used by both governments throughout the sixties. Bank Rate did not fall below $5\frac{1}{2}$ per cent throughout Labour's period of office, and twice reached as high as 8 per cent. At various times, for example after the international monetary crisis in the Autumn of 1968, the commercial banks had ceilings fixed on their lending, especially for personal consumption. The Government also reintroduced special deposits as an instrument of controlling bank lending.

Fiscal policy

Similarly the full range of fiscal measures at the Government's disposal was exploited. Apart from the use of the Budget as a means of soaking up purchasing power and reducing government expenditure, it was necessary for the Government to introduce deflationary fiscal packages at various times of economic crisis. Thus in the 1966 'July measures', which effectively killed the National Plan, the reaction to severe pressure on sterling included the tightening of hire-purchase regulations, the use of the regulator, a proposed surtax surcharge for the next Finance Bill and reductions in public investment. In November 1968 the regulator was again brought into use and this particular package, aimed at 'getting the balance of payments right more quickly',[1] included a new measure, the import

---

[1] One of many similar phrases used by politicians and official publications throughout the sixties.

deposit. 50 per cent of the value of goods had to be paid on most imported goods other than basic foods and raw materials. The goods affected, mainly manufactures were broadly those to which another measure, the 1964–6 temporary import surcharge, had applied. The deposit was returned to the importer 180 days after his original payment, but no interest was paid on what was in effect a short-term loan to the Government.

As might have been expected the Labour Government introduced a Capital Gains Tax soon after its return to power. In the Finance Act of 1965 provision was made for the Government to collect 30 per cent of any capital gain, with certain exceptions including money profit obtained from the sale of one's own house. The same Finance Act also saw the introduction of a new system of taxation of companies, corporation tax replacing income and profits tax. The rate was originally 40 per cent, but was successively increased by $2\frac{1}{2}$ per cent in the Budgets of 1968 and 1969. Gaming and betting has received increasing attention from the Labour Chancellors, but the most remarkable innovation was the Selective Employment Tax introduced in the 1966 Budget and becoming operative in September of that year. Ostensibly this is a tax to encourage economy in the use of labour in the service industries. It was originally paid by all employers at a weekly rate of 25s. for men, 12s. 6d. for women and boys and 8s. for girls. Discrimination against service and construction industries was achieved by giving employers in manufacturing industries not only a refund but a premium, in total 32s. 6d. for men 16s. 3d. for women and boys and 10s. 6d. for girls. There are several neutral industries which received refund but no premium. These include transport, agriculture and the nationalized industries. Various changes have been made in this tax, including regional discrimination in favour of 'Development Areas',[1] but mainly involving increased rates. In 1969, after the increases announced in the Budget, the respective rates were 48s., 24s. and 16s. for men, women and boys, and girls. This tax has caused a great deal of controversy as people have questioned its effectiveness in transferring labour from services to manufactures, and it is presumed exports. It is argued that the extended use of so regressive a tax ill became a Labour Government,[2] but there was little doubt that it was a very effective way of raising

---

[1] See *Regional Planning and the Location of Industry*, pp. 43–6.

[2] An example was the statement by Lord Sainsbury after the 1969 Budget increases in S.E.T. when he called the measure a 'tax on food'.

revenue and as such was likely to remain unless there was a change of government.

Under the 1966 Industrial Development Act, the Government replaced the various investment incentives, which had existed since 1959 for new plant and machinery and for new industrial buildings, with an entirely new system of incentives designed to stimulate investment in those sections of industry and parts of the country where they were most needed. Initial and investment allowances (see page 48) in the key sectors were replaced by cash grants, and industrial building and new plant and machinery which did not qualify for the new grants received higher initial allowances. The scheme concentrated incentives in those sectors where investment was urgently needed because of the contribution made to the balance of payments either by providing exports or saving imports. Discrimination was also used to assist the Development Areas.[1]

The 1969 Budget saw the introduction of a number of new incentives to attract people to national savings. The need for such encouragement had increasingly been argued as alternatives to national savings, particularly unit trusts, had become increasingly popular over the last ten years, with people looking for a reasonably safe way to hedge against inflation. The new contractual savings scheme enabled everyone over the age of sixteen to save up to £10 per month, through deductions from pay or standing orders to banks and the Giro, or cash over the Post Office counter. After five years, savings of £1 per month totalling £60, would be eligible for a £12 tax free bonus. If the money were left for a further two years the bonus would become £24. If money were withdrawn after one year, but before the five years had elapsed, tax free interest of $2\frac{1}{2}$ per cent would be received. The Government was obviously heavily weighting the advantage to the long-term saver and the fact that the rate of return incorporated an element to cover the expected fall in the value of money was an added attraction. There was the danger, however, that this acceptance of the need to compete for funds could have been interpreted as an admission by the Government that it could not control inflation.[2]

---

[1] See *Regional Planning and Location of Industry*, pp. 38–43.

[2] This view, which should not be exaggerated in this context, found favour with the Radcliffe Committee which argued against the introduction of 'index bonds' entailing 'the confession of failure we find so repugnant' see paragraphs 573, 593.

Productivity, prices and incomes

By the beginning of the sixties it was increasingly recognized that the seemingly conflicting objectives of government economic policy could only be achieved within the framework of an incomes policy designed to keep growth of money incomes within the limits of the growth of the national product. If prices were to be stable in a period of full employment and growth, increases in money incomes could only take place as a return for increased productivity. An incomes policy was therefore going to be part of Conservative 'indicative planning' and accordingly a section on Prices and Incomes was found in the N.E.D.C. policy statement, 'Conditions Favourable to Faster Growth'. The Report was careful to state that such a policy could only succeed if it was clear that *all* incomes were to be controlled. This is obviously valid. Organized labour quite rightly sees a 'wages freeze' of the type that had been attempted in the late fifties, as a means of transferring income from wages to profits. Thus in order to obtain the co-operation of the unions there is need to control profits as well as wages. In practice however it is difficult to recognize and control profit increases. Since in simple terms a price increase, wages constant, equals a profit increase, and since changes in price are relatively easy to regulate, emphasis has therefore been given to the control of incomes and *prices*.

Little was in fact done by the Conservatives to implement this policy. In November 1962 the National Incomes Commission was set up to provide advice on claims for income increases in both the public and private sectors but it met with little success for lack of union co-operation. The first public acknowledgement of *combined* agreement to the principle of a prices and incomes policy had to wait for the new administration, when in December 1964 an obviously delighted George Brown signed the Joint Statement of Intent on Productivity, Prices and Incomes along with the representatives of management and unions. This declaration accepted the aims of securing efficient and competitive industry, keeping growth of incomes within the limits of increasing productivity and stabilizing the general price level. Both sides of industry were now committed to co-operate with the Government in pursuing these aims and establishing the machinery necessary to put the policy into practice.

In April 1965 the National Board for Prices and Incomes was established to investigate all questions of prices and incomes referred to it by the Government. Its terms of reference were set out in the White Paper 'Prices and Incomes Policy' published at the same time.

Using the expected rate of growth of national product assumed in the National Plan, which was then being prepared, the White Paper suggested the annual rate of growth of output per head, and therefore the growth of money income to be allowed, to be in the order of 3½ per cent. Exceptional pay increases could be granted in four sets of circumstances where (a) changes in working practices led to increased productivity, (b) the national interest demanded a particular distribution of manpower, (c) existing levels were too low to maintain a reasonable standard of living, and (d) a particular group of workers were receiving less than was comparable elsewhere for similar work.

On price increases the White Paper was less specific. Price increases were to be 'avoided where possible' and 'reduced whenever circumstances permit'. Again there were exceptions where (a) labour productivity could not be raised sufficiently to cover 'normal' wage increases, and there was no margin provided by the possibility of reducing non-labour costs or profits, (b) there were unavoidable increases in non-labour costs such as increases in the price of imported raw materials, and again there was no margin anywhere else, and (c) after everything possible had been done to reduce costs, the firm was not attractive enough to secure the capital required to meet demand. Considering the loopholes provided the N.B.P.I. did well to establish itself immediately as a force to be reckoned with. From the beginning its reports were outspoken and positively critical, obviously reflecting the approach of its exceptionally able chairman, Aubrey Jones, a former Conservative Minister who commanded considerable respect in the business world. His decision to resign in 1969 left a gap that was hard to fill.

In September 1965 the Government announced its intention to introduce legislation in order to make its incomes policy more effective. In the meanwhile arrangements were made for an 'Early Warning System' to operate. Under the system, which was voluntary, specified price increases were notified to the appropriate government department, and wage settlements to the T.U.C. and Ministry of Labour. The Government then had thirty days to decide if it wanted the increase referred to the N.B.P.I. and if this was done there was a further standstill for three months while the Board reported.

In the middle of the following year the Government announced a series of far-reaching measures designed to eliminate the inflationary pressure which was a primary cause of the balance of payments difficulties. These 'July measures' included a standstill on prices and incomes, details of which were incorporated in a Bill placed before

69

Parliament, to enable productivity to catch up with the excessive increases in incomes which had been taking place. There was to be a standstill in prices and incomes, including directors' fees and company distributions, up to December 1966, followed by a further six months of 'severe restraint'. Under Part IV of the Bill, which became law on 12th August, the Government was given reserve powers to give legal support to the standstill should the need arise. This was a temporary provision which was to lapse after twelve months. It did not impose a general statutory standstill on all prices and incomes but was used to ensure that the 'selfish minority'[1] did not benefit at the expense of those who were voluntarily deferring price and wage increases. These reserve powers were used only six times in the period of standstill and little more in the period of severe restraint. The fact that in the period July 1966 to March 1967 the wages index remained constant and the wholesale and retail prices indices rose respectively by only one-third of one per cent and one and three-quarter per cent, and this primarily the result of tax increases, can be taken as an indication of the success of the policy and the co-operation received by the Government from both sides of industry.

In June 1967 a White Paper 'Prices and Incomes Policy after 30th June 1967' indicated that a return was to be made to the original criteria for the regulation of prices and incomes. The early warning system was to continue but there were to be some additional powers for a further twelve-month period. The Government was to receive advance notice of proposed increases in prices or incomes but under the proposed 1967 Prices and Incomes Act the delaying period while reference was made to the N.B.P.I. could be extended to six months. Further, the Government could suspend increases where they were made without early warning or before the Board had reported.

When the Department of Employment and Productivity took over responsibility for the policy in April 1968, another White Paper, 'Productivity, Prices and Incomes Policy in 1968 and 1969' announced a new phase in a policy designed to ensure that rising costs did not cancel out any advantage obtained by the devaluation of the previous autumn. There was to be a ceiling of $3\frac{1}{2}$ per cent on wage, salary and dividend increases. The existing criteria for price changes were still thought to be appropriate, bearing in mind an expected rise in prices in 1968 of 3 per cent due to the Budget. The same exceptions were

---

[1] D.E.A. Report No. 19.

allowed, but particular emphasis was given to the encouragement of productivity agreements. Government support to the voluntary working of the policy was strengthened by increasing the possible period of delay to twelve months. These arrangements were to end in December 1969 but there was as usual provision in the legislation for renewal should this prove necessary.

The continued emphasis given to the Productivity, Prices and Incomes Policy underlined the importance it had as an integral part of Labour Government planning policy. Unfortunately, if inevitably, it became associated with the ever-present need for restraint which undermined so much of what the Government tried to accomplish. The strength of the N.B.P.I. was the potential source of its own destruction unless growth could be achieved and more emphasis could be placed on positive agreements aimed at the encouragement of increased productivity.

Added to those who questioned the viability of such a policy were those who argued that it was not needed anyway, the anti-planners whose opinions received no little boost from the seeming lack of attainment of the Labour Government. They were likely to be the same people who were becoming increasingly worried by the extension in practice of the role of the N.B.P.I. to a point where it might have decided policy. Since the need for objectivity resulted in the Board being a non-representative body, this last concern, at least, was a valid one. It was felt at the time that the position of the N.B.P.I. would be a precarious one should a Conservative Government be returned at the next General Election.

Conclusion

The gradual development of government intervention has nearly always been in belated response to particular need. At each stage in the extension of influence there has always been a rearguard action fought by vested interest. In general terms the experience of the sixties was no exception to this pattern. In order to reconcile the conflicting objectives of the 1944 White Paper the Labour Government particularly felt it necessary to do more than provide a conducive atmosphere and this met with criticism from both sides of industry. From management came accusations that the Government was 'getting in on the act'[1], and from the unions came the refusal to co-operate which led to the abandonment of the controlling legislation

---

[1] Mr John Davies, then Director General of the C.B.I.

71

proposed in the White Paper 'In Place of Strife'. As far as the Labour Government was concerned consultation through recently developed machinery as well as traditional channels, was to be continued and extended as it strove to manage the economy. On one point however there was considerable retraction. Having seen its National Plan effectively destroyed by successive deflationary measures, the Government was careful not to provide rigid growth targets in subsequent publications. Its final policy document[1] gave repeated emphasis to the fact that it was 'not a plan', 'not a blueprint'. In assessing the possible course for the economy up to 1972, it introduced the insurance of a 'wedge-shaped' extrapolation. On the basis of past trends and future government action it gave lower and upper limits for the expected rate of expansion. This was not only a sensible policy in a mixed economy, but an essential one in the atmosphere of continued balance of payments pressure, if planning, thought to be essential by both parties at the end of the fifties, was not to lose further standing.

---

[1] *The Task Ahead, Economic Assessment to 1972*, D.E.A.

9.
1970-1971 TOWARDS A NEW STYLE OF GOVERNMENT

Initial survey

The policy of positive government intervention was to suffer a severe setback with the election of the Conservative Government on 18 June 1970. The electorate had become disenchanted with a Labour administration which had once more, and for too long, been obliged to pursue a policy of tight control and restraint; in this case in order to overcome the country's balance of payments difficulties. At the time of the election increasing unemployment, rising prices, seen by many to be partially the result of an inevitable softening of the Government's attitude towards wage increases, and a temporary setback in the now basically sound trade situation had all combined to give the impression that control had failed. The Conservatives were thus given a mandate to create an atmosphere in which individual freedom, responsibility and effort would reap its just reward.

The new machinery of government

On 15 October 1970 the Conservative Government published a White Paper[1] announcing plans for an extensive reorganization of the machinery of government. Five ministries were to be abolished in creating two new 'super-ministries'; the Department of Trade and Industry and the Department of the Environment. The Department of Trade and Industry (D.T.I.) was formed by the merger of the Ministry of Technology and the Board of Trade. It would also take responsibility for monopolies, mergers and restrictive practices from the Department of Employment and Productivity, which now became simply the Department of Employment. The one responsibility the new department did not inherit was that for civil and military aerospace. This became the responsibility of the newly created Ministry of Aviation Supply. This was an interim measure designed to give the Government time to separate civil and military responsibilities. On

---

[1] 'The Reorganization of Central Government.'

1 May 1971 the Ministry of Aviation Supply was abolished. Responsibility for procurement of defence equipment was undertaken by a new procurement executive under the Secretary of State for Defence, while civil aerospace responsibilities reverted to the D.T.I. (The new Secretary of State for Trade and Industry and President of the Board of Trade was to be Mr John Davies, formerly the Minister of Technology and at one time Director General of the Confederation of British Industry.) The Department of the Environment was formed by the unification of the Ministry of Housing and Local Government, the Ministry of Transport, and the Ministry of Public Works. The new Secretary of State for the Environment was to be Mr Peter Walker, formerly the Minister of Housing and Local Government. A further change occurred with the transfer of the Ministry of Overseas Development to the Foreign and Commonwealth Office. It was finally proposed that a small staff of experts would be established to form a central capability unit within the Cabinet Office. Its task would be to review central policy matters, questioning and challenging departmental decisions. This 'think tank' would be headed by Lord Rothschild, senior scientific executive of the Royal Dutch Shell Group and a Labour peer. Another central unit would analyse and keep a close watch on public expenditure.

The purpose of these changes as announced in the White Paper was to achieve 'less government and better government carried out by fewer people'. The Government intended to withdraw from many areas 'liberating private initiative and placing more responsibility on the individual and less on the State'.

Monetary policy

The Government's overall policy of greater freedom and movement towards the market-place was illustrated in a consultative document[1] published by the Bank of England in May 1971. Various measures were suggested which would act as a basis for discussion with financial institutions. Their aim was to free the banks from some of their former restraints, encourage more competition between them, and incidently bring this country closer to the sort of credit control exercised in Europe. The main proposals were that (i) lending ceilings on banks should be dropped, (ii) the whole banking system should be subject to a reserve requirement of liquid assets equal to $12\frac{1}{2}$ per cent of their sterling balances, (iii) special deposits should continue to be

---

[1] 'Competition and Credit Control.'

an instrument of policy, with perhaps a different percentage for overseas deposits, (iv) the cartel on interest rates should be abandoned, and (v) the lending institutions should be free to respond to market interest rates on each item in their asset structure, although Bank Rate would still be used as an instrument of control.

One limit on the efficacy of monetary policy, the availability of other sources of finance, has been recognized in the proposals to control *all* banks and impose separate percentage rates for special deposits on overseas assets. However, monetary policy has always suffered from the fact that it is far more effective as an instrument of constraint. It will be interesting to see, therefore, if the suggested changes in policy, if implemented, will be any more successful in helping to provide expansion and employment while limiting inflation. At the time of writing restriction on bank lending remains and although money advances have been allowed to expand, in real terms there has been a slight squeeze.

Fiscal policy

The twin Conservative philosophies of less government intervention and greater reward to individual effort obviously meet in the field of public finance. The new Government was committed to less expenditure and could thus use the consequent saving to provide tax relief for the successful. The first announcement of practical measures to implement this policy came in the October 1970 'mini-Budget' in which Mr Anthony Barber, the new Chancellor, announced substantial cuts in the existing programme of public expenditure, including particularly the social services, and accompanying cuts in direct taxation. Much more of the cost of social services was to be borne by the user, although the number eligible for exemption was to be extended. Full discussion of the implications of this move towards selectivity, i.e. concentration of free benefits to those in most need,[1] lies beyond the scope of this book. There is little doubt, however, that many poorer families will suffer hardship as the result of these measures. Those below the poverty line will suffer in that for a variety of reasons they will not ask for benefits to which they are entitled. In any case the poverty line is thought by many to be drawn too low, so that real hardship will be felt by those families whose income is above this line but below the national average wage. Neither, of course, will

---

[1] The most important example being the new Family Income Supplement.

they receive the benefits of the cuts in direct taxation proposed in the Spring Budget, comprising as they did reductions in Income Tax and Surtax, a rise to £12,500 in the exemption limit on estate duty, and the abolition of Short Term Capital Gains Tax. The incentive effect has often been criticized. It is especially difficult to see how these particular measures are relevant to increasing the efforts of the families cited above.

The policy of further encouraging *profitable* enterprise was evident in changes made in investment incentives. Investment grants were abolished immediately, being replaced by a depreciation allowance for plant and machinery enabling 60 per cent of investment expenditure to be written off in the first year, and 25 per cent of the reducing balance in subsequent years. 'Free depreciation' was to be introduced for most new plant and machinery used in the Development Areas, which would also benefit from a continuation of the 40 per cent initial allowance for new industrial buildings and increased building grants. Regional Employment Premiums were not to be retained, however, after the initial seven-year period expired in 1974. 'Free depreciation' was to continue on the total cost of ships. These changes meant that a firm would no longer receive an allowance on new plant whether it expected to make a profit or not. This emphasis on profitable investment led to fears expressed at the time that unless the Government was prepared to make exceptions many receivers of necessary government support, including large engineering companies, shipyards, and aviation companies, might find it difficult to continue in the more competitive atmosphere envisaged in the new proposals.[1]

In the same October speech Mr Barber announced a cut in Corporation Tax from 45 to 42½ per cent, and in agriculture the introduction of a system of import levies accompanied by a reduction in deficiency payments. This last policy is, of course, consistent both with the transfer of the cost of government measures from the general taxpayer to the consumer, and with the movement towards Europe.

The Chancellor continued these policies in the Spring Budget. In the apparently contradictory conditions of steeply rising prices and increasing unemployment he decided to give modest encouragement to consumer demand through further reductions in taxation. In the event these measures were seen to have been an underestimate of the

---

[1] See for example 'Short Term Trends in Mechanical Engineering', N.E.D.C.

amount of stimulus required and so further reflationary measures were introduced in July, the most important being the reduction in purchase tax rates. Apart from a further reduction in Corporation Tax to 40 per cent and the cuts in direct taxation mentioned above, the Spring Budget's main immediate tax proposal was the halving of S.E.T., with the promise of complete abolition in 1973 when a European style Value Added Tax would replace both S.E.T. and Purchase Tax. As for controlling prices it is unlikely that much of the savings in labour costs in the service industries resulting from the cut in S.E.T. will find its way into consumers' pockets. Purchase tax cuts, however, do have a direct effect, and this together with looser hire purchase controls has increased consumer demand. Business confidence was given further encouragement by the increase in the first year depreciation allowance to 80 per cent and by an extension of 'free depreciation' to the service industries in the Development Areas.

At the time of the General Election the Conservatives had argued that one way to reduce taxation was to further encourage saving. It was no surprise therefore when additional incentives to save were announced in the Spring Budget. These were; a single weekly Premium Bond prize of £50,000 to be introduced from August 1971, with the limit on individual holdings raised from £1,250 to £2,000, increases from £10 to £20 in the upper limit on the monthly contributions under S.A.Y.E., and from £500 to £1000 on individual holdings of the decimal issue of National Savings Certificates, and a new issue of British Savings Bonds to be available from May with an increase from £2 to £3 in the tax-free bonus payable at the end of five years.

Productivity, prices and incomes

In December 1969 the Labour Government announced its policy on productivity, prices and incomes for the period following the termination of the existing arrangements. From January 1970 the Government's strict delaying powers over prices and incomes under the 1968 Act would be replaced for a period of up to twelve months by the less rigorous 'notification and standstill' provisions of the 1966 Act. It was also proposed that wage and salary settlements should conform to a 'norm' of $2\frac{1}{2}$ to $4\frac{1}{2}$ per cent per annum. The $3\frac{1}{2}$ per cent ceiling on dividend increases would not be continued, however, after the existing arrangement expired at the end of the year.

Examination of pay and price increases by the N.B.P.I. inevitably involved consideration of wider issues, for example the extent to which a firm or industry made full use of its capacity. On many occasions therefore the work of the N.B.P.I. overlapped that of the Monopolies Commission. The Government thus decided to establish a Commission for Industry and Manpower (C.I.M.) to bring together and develop the work of the N.B.P.I. and the Monopolies Commission. The new Commission would be responsible to the Department of Employment and Productivity. Although the Bill to set up the C.I.M. was published in March 1970 the committee stage had not been completed before the dissolution of Parliament. It was unlikely that the Conservatives, who had continuously expressed doubts as to the effectiveness of 'compulsion', would be sympathetic to the resuscitation of the Bill, involving as it would the acceptance of the constraining policies of the N.B.P.I. In the event they abolished the N.B.P.I. and plans were announced instead to extend the functions of the Monopolies Commission. The scope of the Commission's powers would be widened; for example it would be able to collect information on its own account and examine the nationalized industries. As important, however, was the change in terms of reference which, as might have been expected, gave more emphasis to the role of competition. As well as providing safeguards against the abuse of market power, the Commission would be a 'more effective body for promoting competition throughout the economy'.[1]

Committed as it was to a policy of freedom from restraint the new Government did little to control the sharply increasing rate of price inflation. The size of wage increases was also becoming alarmingly high, particularly in the private sector. Some effort was made by the Government to bring pressure to bear on the size of wage increases in the public sector, for example in settlement of the postal dispute, but Opposition calls for an overall incomes policy were dismissed. An initiative on prices was taken by the C.B.I. in the summer of 1971 when it announced that a 5 per cent ceiling was to be placed on price increases proposed by its larger members over the next year. The Chancellor later announced that the major nationalized industries would also comply with this voluntary restraint.

Implications for private industry

The new Government's attitude to industry was made quite clear in the Queen's Speech at the opening of the new session of Parliament. Enterprise was to be encouraged by 'liberating industry from unnecessary intervention by Government'. Thus the D.T.I. was estab-

---

[1] Mr John Davies.

lished to assist British industry in providing an atmosphere in which firms could 'operate as freely as possible to their own individual advantage'.[1]

The first practical proposals came in the Chancellor's October 1970 mini-Budget. Apart from the fiscal policies already outlined several measures were announced which affected industry directly. The Industrial Reorganization Corporation was to be dissolved at the end of May 1971. It was argued that the I.R.C. was an inappropriate government instrument in that there was little need to engineer mergers and that it was in any case irrational to provide money from public funds in a period of credit squeeze. However, in July 1971 it was announced that a new agency would be formed to partially fill the gap. It would obtain its capital from both public and private sources indicating that it would be used less as an instrument of policy and more as a simple supplier of credit. Further cuts were to be made in Government expenditure on the support of industry and technology generally, including the phasing out of the British Productivity Council and reductions in expenditure on Research Councils. In short industry was to receive less support in an attempt to promote profitable enterprise. A corollary to this was that un-profitable enterprise would no longer be supported artificially, a point emphasized by Mr Davies in the Parliamentary debate following the proposals when he stated that the Government had no intention of helping 'lame ducks'.

In general the Government has tended to be true to its policy. In 1970 the ailing Mersey Docks and Harbour Board were refused bridging finance by the Government. This resulted in the resignation of top management and, with capital debts of over £80 million, the raising of port dues in stages by 45 per cent. In May 1971 it was announced that there would be no State backing for a nuclear merchant vessel. In the same month doubts were expressed about continued support for the National Building Agency, set up in 1964 to encourage industrialized building techniques. The following month saw the beginning of withdrawal of support from the British film industry.

The Government's emphasis on profitability gives rise to obvious criticism on social grounds. It is argued by many commentators that in some cases social benefits to be gained from the retention of employment more than outweight the private cost to the Exchequer

---

[1] 'The Reorganization of Central Government.'

in supporting unprofitable enterprise. This view is very relevant to the case of Upper Clyde Shipbuilders Ltd, where the Government refused to give more financial support to the Labour Government created consortium which had already received £24·8 million from central funds, despite the fact that local unemployment levels were desperately high and the decision could mean the loss of as many as 6,000 jobs.[1] At the time of writing the Government has forced the liquidation of the company but is providing funds to enable the company to continue until reconstruction takes place on a more economically viable basis. This will be achieved by concentration of production at two or at most three of the four yards involved, standardization of ship production, reform of management, and more productive and realistic working arrangements with employees. It will be interesting to see how the Government pursues this policy against calls for nationalization by the Opposition and a 'work in' at all four yards organized by the shop stewards.

Despite general adherence to its policy the Government has occasionally made exceptions. In July 1971 a selective grant scheme worth £50 million was introduced to encourage mineral exploration in Britain. Social considerations must have been partially responsible for the Government's increased assistance to Harland and Wolff, the Belfast shipbuilding and engineering group. The company, which was already in receipt of over £20 million and in temporary State control since early 1971, received a further £7 million in July. It has a one million ton building dock which is the largest in the world, but more important, it is Belfast's biggest single employer with a workforce of ten thousand.

The greatest test of the Government's resolve not to help 'lame ducks', however, came with the impending collapse of Rolls Royce at the end of 1971. In October 1969 the Labour Government had granted the company £47 million launching aid for the *RB 211–22* aero engine. This had been chosen by the American Lockheed company to power its *L1011 TriStar* airbus. A further £10 million had been provided by the I.R.C. to offset the burden of development on the company's cash reserves, and another £10 million had been promised for April 1971. Further cost increases, however, forced the company to ask for more money in the autumn of 1970. Seemingly against its policy the Government announced in November that a further £60 million would be made available, £18 million of which

---

[1] *The Times*, 30 July 1971.

would be provided by the commercial banks. There would, however, be no further instalment from the I.R.C. As a condition of support the Government required an independent check of the company's accounts and an interim limit on dividend payments on ordinary share capital.

In justifying its action in this case the Government argued that the company, which had been the only major manufacturer of aero engines since 1966, was vital to national defence and also to airforces, civil airlines and private operators throughout the world. Similar arguments were used when in February 1971 the major part of the firm was nationalized to form Rolls Royce (1971) Ltd. The company's financial position had worsened as the result of increasing costs, compensation to Lockheed for expected late delivery, and the inadequacy of the original fixed price contract. Its prospects had not been helped, however, when the Government decided not to provide launching aid for the *BAC 3–11* nor rejoin the *A 300B* European airbus project, both of which would have used a modified *RB211* engine. The Government negotiated a new contract with Lockheed which was itself in financial difficulties, but the future of both companies remained in doubt until in August 1971 the United States Government finally guaranteed the loans Lockheed required to continue the production of the *TriStar*.

The Government have shown great determination in pursuit of their policy to give less support to industry but have found that there are circumstances where support is necessary. There is no doubt that other similar situations will arise and on those occasions the Government might do well to consider straightforward subsidy as a cheaper alternative to liquidation followed by private or public rationalization. It was estimated, for example, by Sir Joseph Lockwood, former Chairman of the I.R.C., that this would have been the case with Rolls Royce.

A new policy for the nationalized industries

In a speech to the Conservative Party Conference in 1970 Mr Davies, then Minister of Technology, announced that the Government's attitude to the nationalized industries was to be essentially one of 'disengagement'. Three practical measures would be taken to achieve this. In the first place peripheral activities would be shed, for example the Electricity Boards could sell their showrooms, the National Coal Board its brickworks. Secondly, there would be less Ministerial control. This would prove more difficult to achieve in that there existed a great deal of ministerial intervention and this appeared to be increasing. Of the reasons for intervention the most important are (i) manipulation in furtherance of government policy, e.g. controlling investment programmes to take account of inflationary pressure, (ii) use in support of British industry, e.g. the airlines have at times been forced to buy British planes they did not want, and (iii) control of pricing policies not only because nationalized industries are monopolies but also more positively for social reasons. Finally private capital would be attracted. This could be done in one of two ways, either by selling the concern entirely or selling a minority shareholding – the B.P. formula.[1] The presence of private capital would give the industry greater power to resist government pressure, but it would only be forthcoming if the nationalized industries made themselves more attractive. They would thus be encouraged to pursue more commercial policies, including charging higher prices.

Various measures have been taken to implement this new policy. In 1970 a second force airline[2] was given the profitable West African routes taken from B.O.A.C. in an attempt to introduce stronger domestic competition into the industry. It seems likely that other routes will also be transferred. The Government also proposed that a holding board would be established for the two State airlines to see if complete merger was necessary in the interests of rationalization. The Coal Industry Bill introduced in November 1970 and which raised the statutory deficit of the industry from £50 million to £75 million (£100 million if necessary) also contained a clause ordering a review of the Coal Board's non-colliery activities to be presented within twelve months. In December 1970 a Bill was introduced to apply the BP formula to the fuel division and isotope laboratories of the Atomic Energy Authority. Initially the separate companies would be owned by the Authority but private capital would subsequently be accepted up to the 49 per cent maximum. This Bill had originally been introduced by the Labour Government but had been lost to the timing of the General Election. In June 1971 Lunn-Poly the State-owned travel group was sold to Cunard for £100,000. Also to be sold are Thomas Cook and Son and the State-owned breweries, public houses and hotels in Carlisle, Cromarty and Gretna. An example of

---

[1] Up to 49 per cent private equity holding as in British Petroleum, formerly the Anglo-Persian Oil Co., see page 17.

[2] British Caledonian, formed when Caledonian took over B.U.A. in October 1970 for £7 million.

the move to less interference occurred when the nationalized industries accepted the 5 per cent price initiative of the C.B.I. They were assured that as a result their investment programmes would not suffer and that price restraint would not lead to more control over their day to day management.

Conclusion

The above summary of recent Government withdrawal from some of its industrial responsibilities should not give the impression that industry will soon be free of the Government altogether. It is important to remember that the Government is concerned to a greater or lesser extent in a wide variety of functions affecting all aspects of industry. Many of these have already been mentioned, but it is worth quickly summarizing the main points of contact at this stage, if only to reinforce the argument that the Government's presence cannot be ignored and that a degree of planning is necessary in order to avoid disruption as the result of government action.

There is, of course, the direct contact provided by the sponsoring departments and through the N.E.D.C. and the E.D.C.s.[1] Direct contact of a different sort is provided by the trade that takes place between private industry and state and municipal enterprise. With 30 per cent[2] of the Gross National Product spent on goods and services and gross fixed investment by the public sector, this could be used as an extremely effective instrument of policy. In practice it is rarely considered, and against such things as the Fair Wages Clause (see page 13), the placing of government contracts to provide employment in low activity areas, and the recently announced £160 million to be spent on infrastructure to provide employment in the depressed regions, must be set situations in which it could be argued that the Government is too passive. For example, a rationalized pharmaceutical industry which did not duplicate research would be able to charge less for the drugs it provided for the N.H.S. There are finally the exceptional circumstances, as with the Ferranti case, where the Government, far from being in control of the situation, might have seemed to be exploited by private industry. In this

---

[1] Although as part of its current policy the Government disbanded the E.D.C.s for rubber, paper, the Post Office, hosiery, and food in November 1970.

[2] This figure does not include transfer payments which brings total public expenditure nearer to 55 per cent of G.N.P.

country it is accepted by most people that it is not desirable for the Government to use its trading and investment decisions to further overall economic policy, at any rate not in peacetime. For any government wishing to increase its hold on the economy, however, it stands out as an effective and readily available means of control.

More acceptable to most is the Government's role as regulator of various sectors of the economy. Thus each type of company is subject to restrictions on for example its formation, its degree of liability in the event of liquidation, which process itself is very closely regulated by the D.T.I. in conjunction with the courts, its treatment of shareholders, its location, and the disposal of its waste. Other economic organizations such as Building Societies and Provident Societies are regulated under specific Acts of Parliament. The Government also regulates the conditions of existence of the trade unions. Under the new Industrial Relations Act it is of course proposed that this regulation is to be extended and reinforced by legal sanctions, although, as indicated elsewhere, current union attitudes seem to indicate that these might be difficult to implement in practice. Where collective bargaining has failed to raise wages and improve working conditions the Government has provided the machinery, so that for example, statutory wage fixing applies to over 5 million workers and legislation covers hours of work, health, and safety in a wide variety of industries. Since the last war the Government has introduced measures to regulate the detrimental aspects of monopoly, merger and restrictive trading agreements. Industry is markedly affected by the Government's international policy as the result not only of direct trading agreements but also political measures with inherent trading implications. Finally the Government gives protection to the individual as a consumer. Despite legislation on resale price maintenance, protection against high-pressured salesmanship, especially involving the signing of hire-purchase agreements, for which there is now the possibility of retraction within a specified time limit, weights and measures regulation, the 1969 Trade Descriptions Act and the provision of advisory Consumer Councils by the Nationalized Industries, it is still felt by many that the consumer is too often exploited. To be fair to the retailer, much of the blame lies with the consumer; if he were to acquiesce less in the buying situation he would get a better bargain. Given the need for protection, however, the Government's recent decision to discontinue its grant to the Consumer Council was disappointing. That 'vigorous competition is the best safeguard for the consumer'[1] is a doubtful premise.

Most acceptable to industry is the Government's role in providing 'a stimulating and stable economic framework within which enterprise can flourish without undue interference'.[2] In practice this involves a great deal of government activity. The Government provides finance for industry in various specified circumstances. For example the gap in the availability of long-term finance for firms too large for the commercial banks and not large enough for the new issues market has been partially closed since the war by the establishment of the Government-promoted Industrial and Commercial Finance Corporation. A similarly sponsored Finance Corporation for Industry provides temporary finance for new or expanding industries unable to raise long-term capital through the usual channels. There are circumstances where capital equipment is made available by the Government. This occurs primarily in war time, but in the aircraft industry particularly there is still a sizeable proportion of government-owned capital equipment, and part of the Government's location of industry policy involves the letting of government-built factories at attractive rates. Further financial assistance is given in the form of subsidies. An obvious example is the support given to agriculture. A less obvious case of government assistance is the element of hidden subsidy in the money provided for research and development in the defence industries, much of which has a commercial application in civil industry. Finally, the Government provides money as an inducement to industry to follow policy thought desirable in the national interest. Employment is provided as the Government encourages industry to move to less active areas, exports are promoted by the Government's insurance scheme, investment and growth are stimulated by various fiscal measures and rationalization is brought about by money provided, most recently through the Industrial Reorganization Corporation.

Other ways in which the Government assists industry include promotion of research, protection of domestic industry against overseas competition, sponsorship of rationalization schemes, establishment

---

[1] The Queen's Speech on the opening of the new Parliament, 2 July 1970.

[2] John Davies, when Director General of the C.B.I. in the Sir George Earle Memorial Lecture given in December 1966 and reprinted in the *Three Banks Review*, July 1967.

of marketing boards, provision of employment services, including industrial training, of consultative and arbitrative machinery in case of breakdown in collective bargaining, and finally encouragement of efficiency at all levels, from management to shop floor, in an attempt to increase productivity.

The Government asks surprisingly little in return for all this money spent; the policies of the individual firms are seldom questioned and no equity interest is demanded. There are circumstances where, for example, the provision of employment can in itself be considered return enough in social terms for money lent or given, but there is much in the argument that a firm which would be unprofitable but for government subsidy, should at least provide a return to the Government on the money it has spent. Private profit has after all been received in a situation where the rule of the market would give none. There are of course those who argue further that if private enterprise cannot provide employment, reasonable price levels or other socially desirable ends, then it is the Government's duty to provide them itself, not to make it possible for the private sector to do so artificially.

This list of government enterprise, regulation and promotion is indeed an impressive one. Together with monetary and fiscal measures, however, it constitutes to most people the accepted function of government as it endeavours to achieve economic objectives which have changed little since their first official appearance in the 1944 White Paper. Where conflict does arise is over the extension of government influence, of which the essays in planning in the sixties were an example. Consultation through, for example, the E.D.C.s was originally heralded by industry as a way in which the Government could 'improve and refine that framework wherein private enterprise might prosper'. To the Government, however, it was partially a means of obtaining information on which to base more positive policy which industry had no part in determining. Industry is sometimes, therefore, reluctant to provide such information. Mr John Davies, when he was Director General of the C.B.I. suggested that a way out of this difficulty would be for consultation to be replaced by partnership, so that industry would be willing to disclose more detail in return for some say in decision taking. It must be remembered, however, that the requirements of industry are not the only things the Government has to consider in formulating policy. Decision taking is the task of an elected government, and though this must be done in consultation with all groups concerned, in the final event it is the Government's responsibility alone. Lack of co-operation or hostility from a particular quarter certainly reduces the chance of a policy being successful, but the answer is not to give the recalcitrant sector a say in decision taking, rather to encourage its co-operation which can only lead to everyone's benefit.

At the present time the Government is moving away from central direction. This is a natural response to the private industrialist's suspicion of 'socialist' policies, but is also a reaction against the failure of planning to provide growth throughout the nineteen sixties. In a period of rapidly increasing prices the main criticism of the Government's approach must be that it should not have abandoned central control of prices and incomes. Without the stability created by such a policy it is difficult to see how the new atmosphere being created by the Government will be successful in stimulating efficiency and a rate of economic growth comparable with other industrialized nations.

BIBLIOGRAPHY

A Concise Economic History of Britain: From Earliest Times to 1750,
Sir John Clapham, C.U.P.

A Concise Economic History of Britain: From 1750 to Recent Times,
W. H. B. Court, C.U.P.

A History of Economic Thought, Eric Roll, Faber.

An Economic History of England, 1870–1939, W. Ashworth, Methuen.

The Development of the British Economy, S. Pollard, Arnold.

Economic Survey, 1919–1939, W. Arthur Lewis, Unwin University
Books.

A History of Economic Change in Britain, R. S. Sayers, O.U.P.

Abstract of British Historical Statistics, Mitchell and Deane, C.U.P.

The British Economy 1945–50, Worswick and Ady (ed.), O.U.P.

British Economic Policy Since the War, A. Shonfield, Penguin.

The Stagnant Society, M. Shanks, Penguin.

The Treasury under the Tories, S. Brittain, Penguin.

The Innovators, M. Shanks, Pelican.

Managing the British Economy, R. Bailey, Hutchinson.

Britain's Economic Prospects: A Brooking's Institution Study,
Richard E. Caves and associates, George Allen & Unwin.

Government and Industry in Britain, J. W. Grove, Longmans.

The Structure of Industry in Britain, G. C. Allen, Longmans.

British Industries and their Organisation, G. C. Allen, Longmans.

British Industry, Dunning and Thomas, Hutchinson.

Economic Organisation of Modern Britain, N. Branton, English
Universities Press.

Economics of Industrial Organisation, Beacham and Williams, Pitman.

Growth through Industry, I.E.A.

Growth in the British Economy, P.E.P., George Allen & Unwin.

Planning for Growth, P.E.P.

Inquest on Planning in Britain, P.E.P.

Thrusters and Sleepers – A Study of Attitudes in British Management,
P.E.P.

Britain's Economic Performance, Industrial Policy Group.

Government Expenditure, Industrial Policy Group.

The National Plan, John Brunner, I.E.A.

Economic Fact and Fantasy, G. C. Allen, I.E.A.
Economic Planning and Democracy, Firmin Oulès, Penguin.

Official Publications
Britain. Official Handbook, H.M.S.O.
Committee on the Working of the Monetary System (Radcliffe), H.M.S.O.
Growth of the U.K. Economy to 1966, N.E.D.C., H.M.S.O.
Conditions Favourable to Faster Growth, N.E.D.C., H.M.S.O.
The National Plan, D.E.A., H.M.S.O.
The Task Ahead. Economic Assessment to 1972, D.E.A., H.M.S.O.

D.E.A. Progress Reports.
Treasury Information Division Economic Progress Reports.

Bank Reviews
'The Perils of Planning', John Jewkes, *Three Banks, June 1965*.
'Government Support for Research and Development', K. Grossfield, *National Prov., February 1967*.
'Industry and Government', John Davies, *Three Banks, June 1967*.
'Planning and Fiscal Strategy', Sir Robert Shone, *National Prov., August 1967*.
'The N.E.D.C. after Six Years', Basil Taylor, *Westminster, February 1968*.
'The "Neddy" Experiment – A New Approach to Planning', *Midland, February 1968*.
'The British Disease and its Cure', Graham Hutton, *National Prov., May 1968*
'Prospect for Faster Growth in Britain', Balls and Burns, *National West., November 1968*.
'Why we need a Prices Policy', Joan Mitchell, *Lloyds, April 1969*.
'The Planning Dialogue', H. F. R. Catherwood, *National West., May 1969*.
'An Incomes Policy to Stop Inflation', Professor Sidney Weintraub, *Lloyds, January 1971*.
'Why Neddy Survived', Sir Frederick Catherwood, *Lloyds, April 1971*.
'It Could Happen Here', Bernard Hollowood, *National West., May 1971*.
'Why We Need Economic Growth', Professor W. Beckerman, *Lloyds, October 1971*.

EXAMINATION QUESTIONS

The questions below are taken from G.C.E. advanced level and university entrance examinations.
1. What useful meaning, if any, can be attached to the word 'mercantilism'? (London).
2. 'Adam Smith, spokesman for the interests of the manufacturers.' Comment (Cambridge).
3. 'The age of laisser-faire.'
   'A period of increasing government intervention in almost every sphere of the economy.'
   How do you reconcile these views of the nineteenth century? (London).
4. Why were the demands for the protection of manufacturing industry unsuccessful in the years 1880–1914? (London).
5. Why was direct taxation used less extensively by British governments before 1914 than after? (London).
6. Account for the growth of State intervention in industry in the period 1918–39 (London).
7. Discuss the view that government measures in aid of British industry in the 1930s were based on a desire for business stability rather than economic growth (London).
8. Why has the average size of business undertakings increased since 1914? (London).
9. What were the main economic problems facing the government in 1945? What solutions were adopted down to 1950? (London).
10. Is there an alternative to 'stop–go' policies? (London).
11. 'The failure of the Labour Government since 1964 results from a refusal to acknowledge the forces of the market.' Discuss (Oxford).
12. Discuss the use of planning as a means of raising a country's rate of growth. Illustrate your answer by the experience of the United Kingdom (London).
13. 'The problem of the 1970s is not whether to plan, but how to plan.' What form of economic planning machinery would you adopt? (Oxford).

INDEX